Wedding Photography
Improve Quickly

by Bill Collins

Black and White Print Edition

Published by Bill Collins

Editor: Jasmine Flower Editing

EAN#: 978-0-9904874-8-7

ISBN#: 0990487482

Some of the content of this book also appears in my other book: ***Wedding Photographer: A 45-Year Career,*** **which is a memoir written just for non-photographers to enjoy, by getting to join me on my rollicking romp down memory lane.**

http://www.amazon.com/Wedding-Photographer-45-Year-Bill-Collins-ebook/dp/B00OWEYAL0

Which version is right for you?

This version, ***Wedding Photography*** **Improve Quickly**, offers instruction and advice on how to quickly become a pro wedding photographer, by avoiding long and steep learning curves. It may prove difficult for some non-photographers to fully understand all the information given. Non-photographers are encouraged to read ***Wedding Photographer: A 45-Year Career. http://www.amazon.com/Wedding-Photographer-45-Year-Bill-Collins-ebook/dp/B00OWEYAL0***

Do you see your picture in this book?

If you see your picture in this book and would like me to remove it, please email me at proweddingphotos@yahoo.com.

These are photos I am proud of having taken. Having them displayed here should also be considered an honor.

When they hired me, all brides and grooms signed contracts that essentially stated that they release and grant to Bill Collins the rights to use any and all of the photos he takes at their wedding and reception for Bill Collins' own sample display, for advertising purposes, or for any other purposes that Bill Collins sees fit to use these photos. However, I realize that some of these couple may no longer be married and may not want their photos to appear in print. That is the reason I offer to remove their photos and replace them with those of other couples.

Dedication:

I dedicate this book to my wife, Sue, whom I love dearly, as much as life itself. She even jogged my memory on a few of the stories that I had nearly forgotten about.

And to the memory of my mother, Oma Richie Collins, who made the world a better place to live while she was here. As sweet a woman as you'll ever meet.

Bill

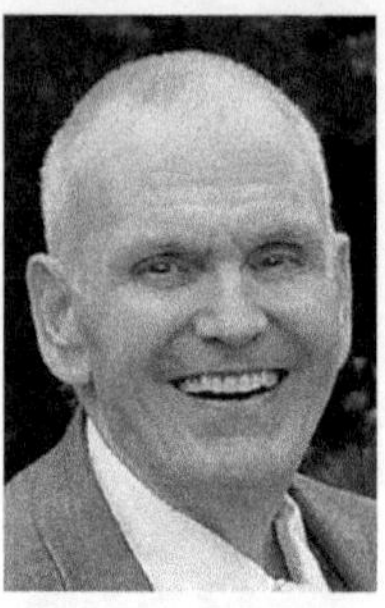

Author's Biography:

Bill Collins is currently a semi-retired wedding photographer. He was formerly a full time pro weddings-only photographer serving the Indianapolis-Cincinnati-Dayton, Ohio regional wedding markets, with 45-years experience as a wedding photographer.

Bill was born in Connersville, Indiana and graduated from CHS in 1963, with almost double the number of credits required to graduate, while managing to skip his Junior year.

He was a top wedding photographer in Connersville for about twenty years. In the 1980s, he moved to Richmond, Indiana, where he owned and operated Bill Collins Photography, at 315 NW L Street, for more than a quarter of a century. During the final fifteen years of his career, he only photographed weddings, averaging a wedding a week year around, by serving mostly big city brides throughout Indiana, Western Ohio and Northern Kentucky.

Bill was formerly a Professional Photographers of America member for many years, who studied at Winona International School of Professional Photography, which is owned by the PPA. He received training by several of the top Master Photographers in the United States throughout his career, in order to make sure his style and abilities were always up to date. Bill is currently living in Greens Fork, Indiana, with Sue, his wife of many years, and their two pet cats.

Facebook Pages for Bill Collins:
https://www.facebook.com/pages/Wedding-Photographer/260780837464089?ref=bookmarks
https://www.facebook.com/bill.collins.12139

Goodreads.com profile for Bill Collins:
https://www.goodreads.com/author/show/8302599.Bill_Collins

Author's website: http://retiredweddingphotog.weebly.com

Table of Contents

Prologue

I presume you purchased this book because you are wanting to be, or trying to be, a better professional wedding photographer. I am at the other end of that scale, being semi-retired after a 45-year career as a wedding photographer in the Midwest regional markets, serving Indianapolis, Cincinnati and Dayton, Ohio. I have a lifetime of knowledge, learning, advice and experiences to share with you.

From my unique vantage point, there really doesn't seem that much that people need to learn to become a good wedding photographer. I want to help guide you in your learning, so you go down the most easily traversed straight road towards knowing what you are doing, while helping you avoid all those dangerous steep learning curves along the way.

I've included my Top 5 Vital Business Documents for you that cover about every facet of the dealing with clients. Be sure to check them out and feel free to use them to help you avoid having to reinvent the wheel. Chapter 1 gives you a road map you can follow to learn and improve quickly.

Chapter 2: Posing Groups Like a Pro, passes on what I was taught by Master Photographers about formal group posing. It is packed with the kind of info that beginners aren't likely to easily discover on their own. Chapter 3 features my "90 Day Get Better Quick Challenge".

Take a peek into my world!

According to my wife, I always took on a totally different persona when I slipped on my suit to go photograph a wedding. When the suit was on and it was time for me to leave for the wedding, I sort of became... Mr. Professional Wedding Photographer Man -- a sort of super hero: calm, cool, confident, capable and unflappable – the sort of man who would always be able to get the job done.

On one occasion, I actually caught a bride as she fell from an elevated altar once, preventing her from possible injury. She had lost her footing and came tumbling right towards me. I was standing at the bottom of the three or four steps leading up to the altar, photographing her, and was able to catch her around the waist with my free arm as she tumbled down the stairs while my other hand safely held my camera.

During the final third of my 45 year career, I was privileged enough to share in and photograph hundreds and hundreds of big city brides' most important day throughout all of Indiana, the western half of Ohio and the northern part of Kentucky. The best I can figure, I ended up photographing over a thousand weddings during my career.

I always thought of myself as just a "meat and potatoes" type of wedding photographer. I was not one of those champagne and caviar type of wedding photographers, the type who are nearly world-famous in their reputations. I was just like numerous other hardworking professional wedding photographers in the nation who ply their trade weekend after weekend, simply doing their jobs efficiently and well. I was more of a well trained and experienced craftsman than an artist.

After struggling to make a living for about fifteen years in my local Richmond, Indiana, market as a full-time, studio owner/photographer, I amazed myself when I moved up to servicing all of Indiana, the western half of Ohio, and northern Kentucky as a full-time, weddings-only photographer and actually succeeded at it. Boy, did things change for me then! I had hoped to succeed financially on photographing solely weddings and abandoning studio photography, as I was having a difficult time doing that in the small local market I was in. There is quite a bit if difference between hoping and doing.

Everyone has memories of their wedding day; after all, it is supposed to be the happiest day of their lives. As a wedding photographer, I got to enjoy countless memories from all of those weddings I was privileged enough to photograph, and I am thankful to have had these experiences.

Most people don't have a clue what goes on in the life of a full-time professional wedding photographer, and I believe you are going to really enjoy learning about some of the hairy experiences that I encountered. I don't claim every wedding photographer's experiences are going to be anywhere near the same as mine, of course.

I write about many of my humorous encounters in the closing chapters of this book. You will read tales about a ceremony in a cemetery and a different reception in a cemetery, the "best dog," two tales about cats, the snake, and the horses.

Oh, the people I have met along the way, and the people I've had to deal with! Some of them are almost unbelievable, and some I would just as soon forget. Thankfully, the vast majority of them were simply wonderful.

If I were to give this book a rating as though it were a movie, I would probably rate it PG, as there are a fistfight mentioned and even a tiny hint of sex.

All the images in this book were pulled from snapshots of my now-defunct website, accessed through Archive.org's Way Back Machine. There is no way I could have located all of them individually within my extensive digital image files. Working from files pulled from the internet makes it difficult for all these photos to be as sharp as they would have been, if taken from the digital originals.

Many of the images appearing in this book were taken with the Nikon's first generation pro DSLR camera, the D1. Sometimes I found it really difficult to get properly saturated images from this first generation digital camera. Image quality improved greatly with second, third and fourth generation models.

Let the learning and the fun begin!

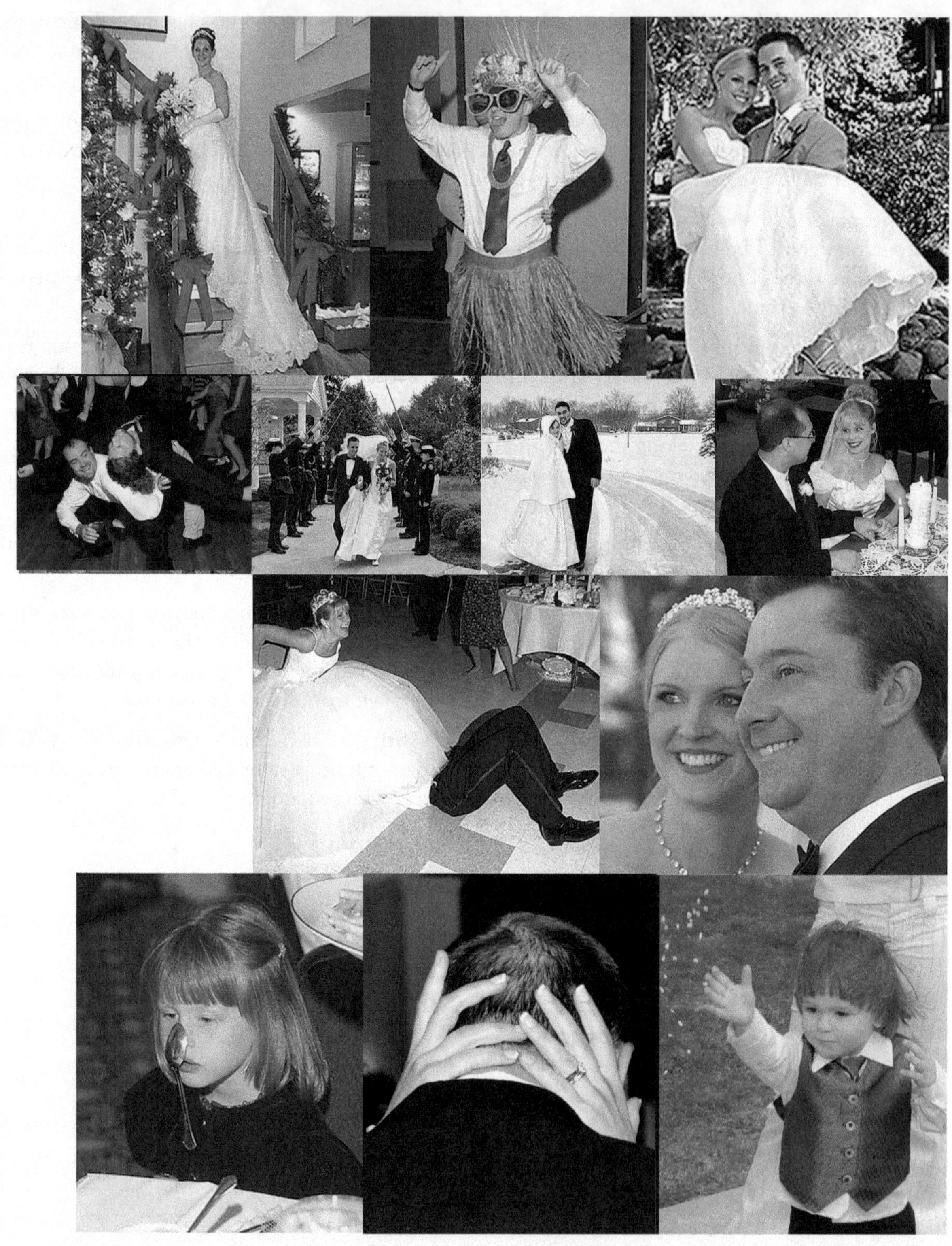

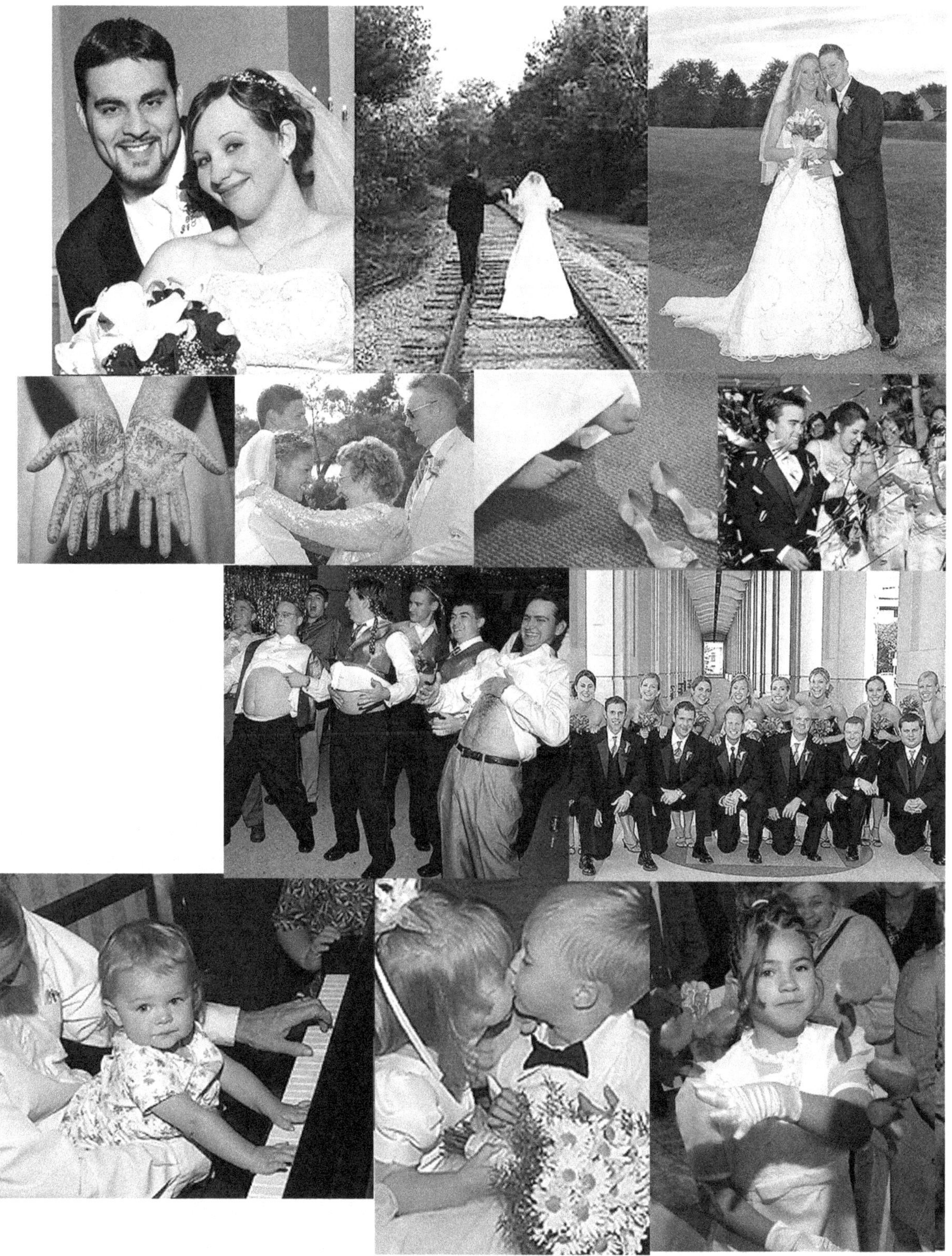

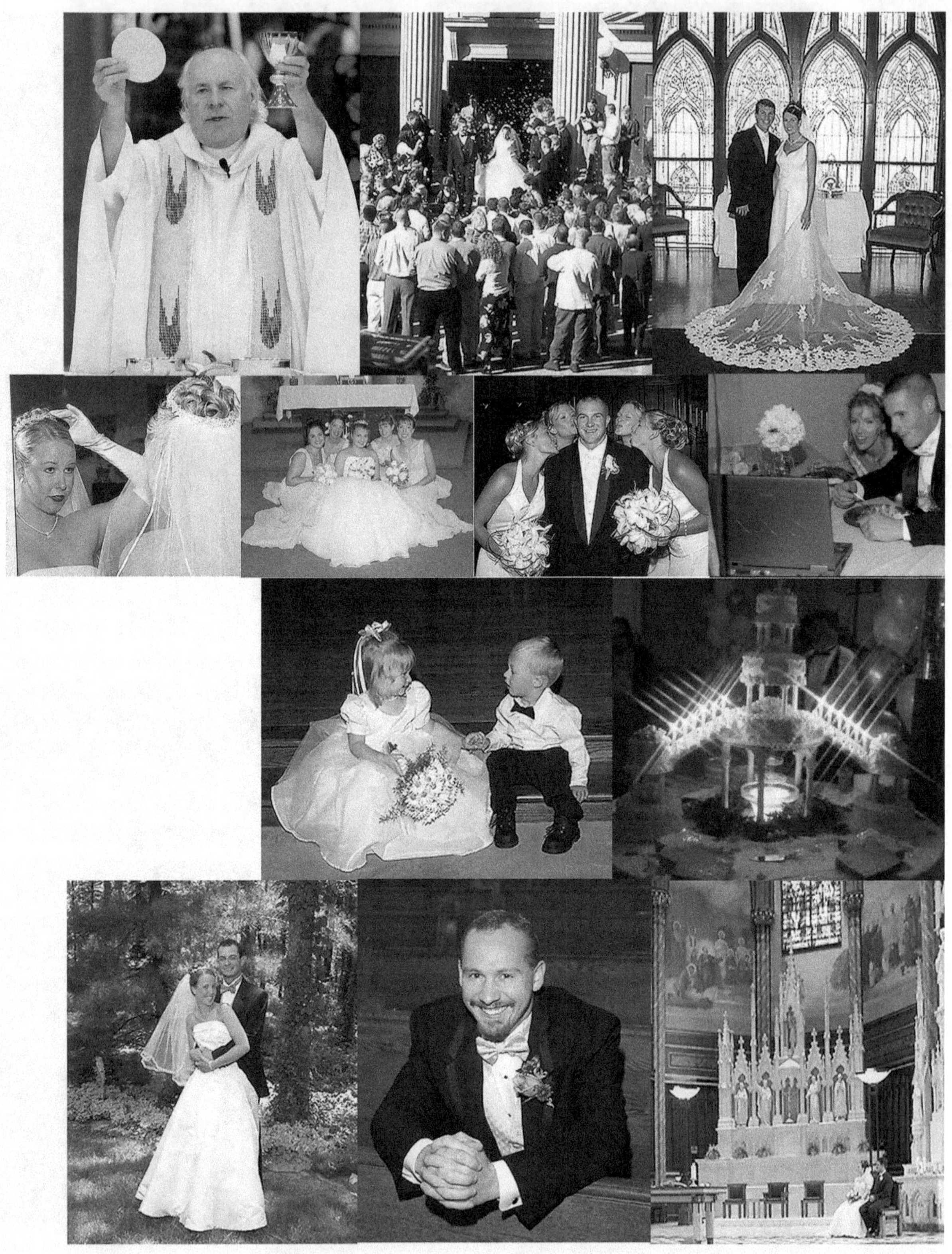

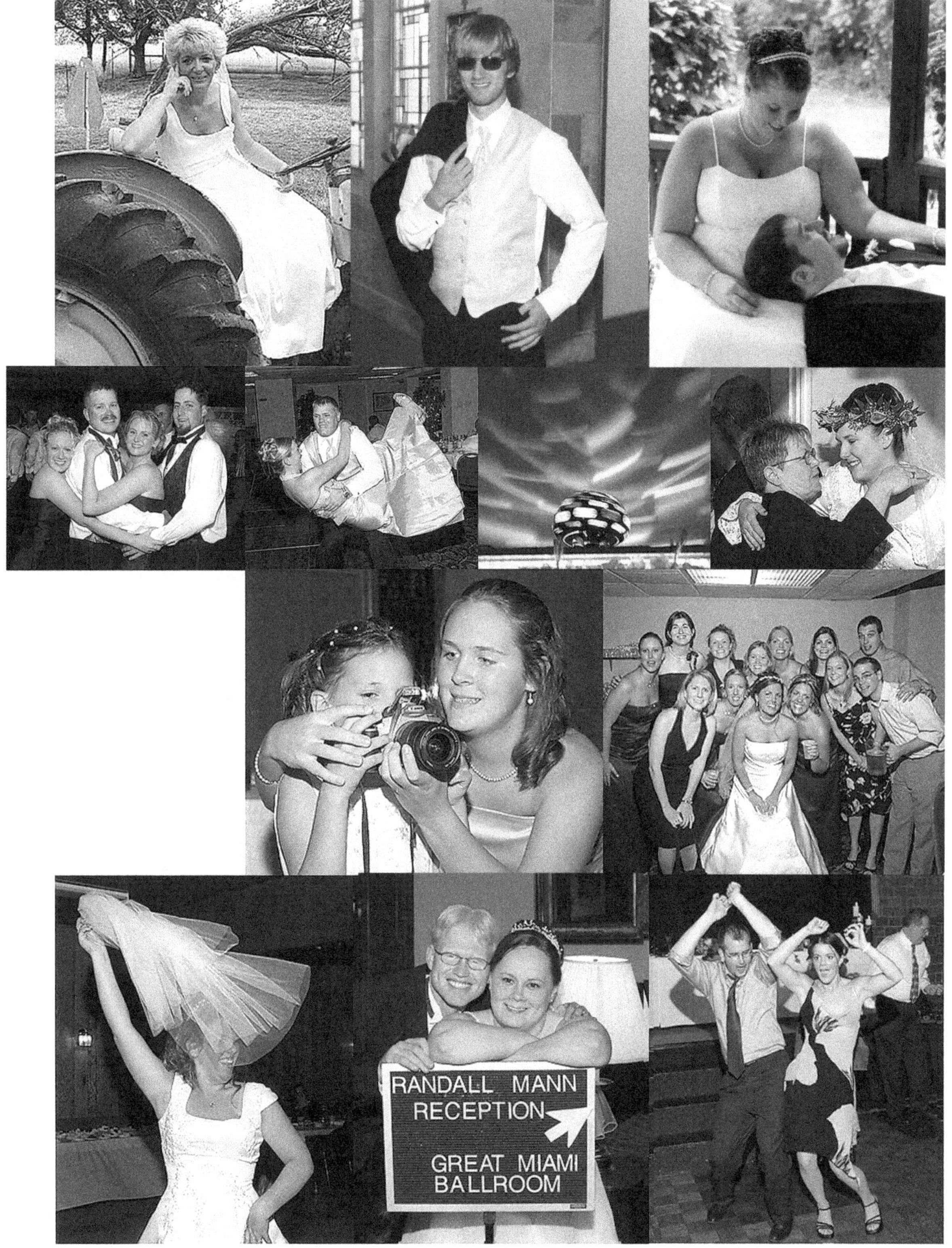
RANDALL MANN
RECEPTION
GREAT MIAMI
BALLROOM

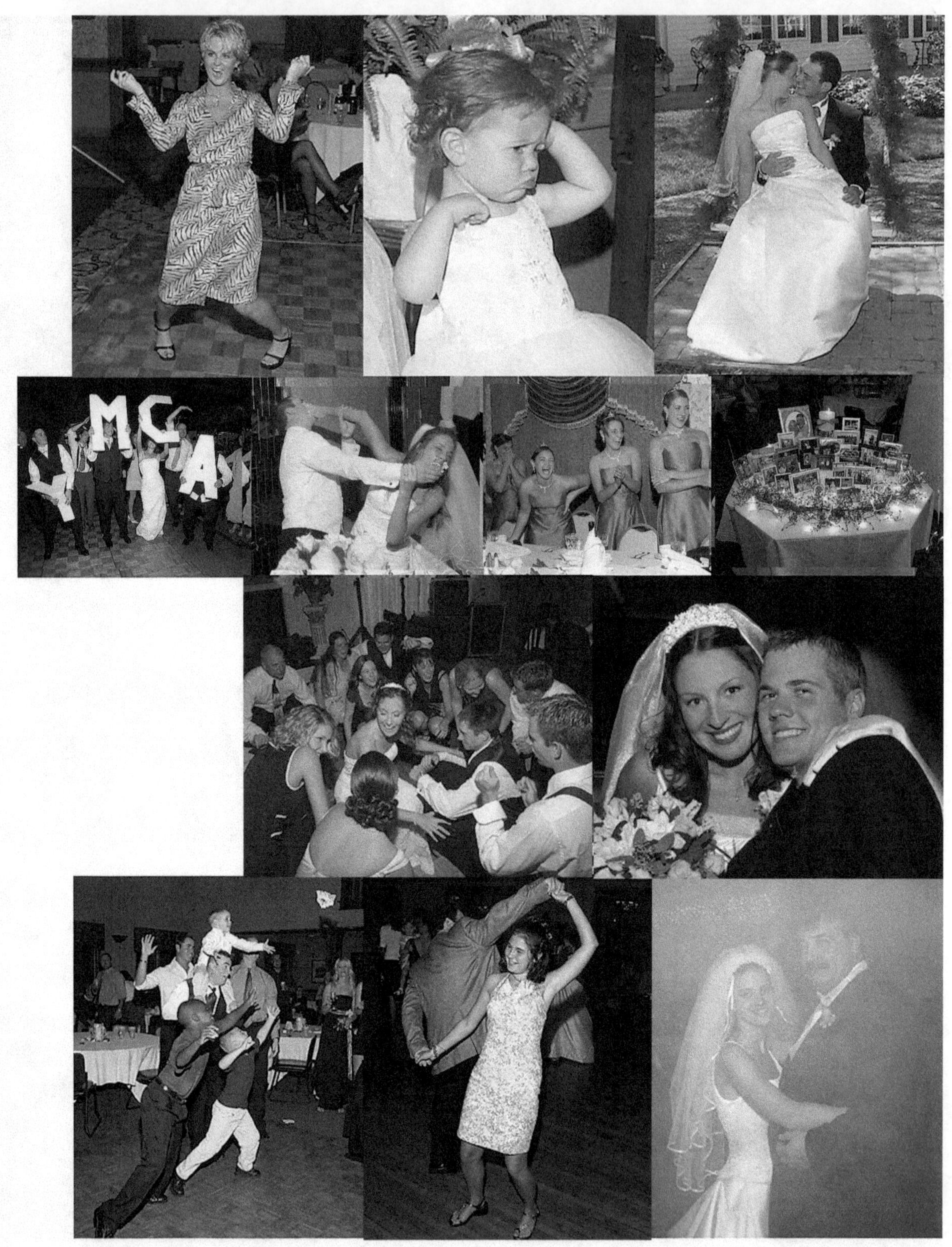

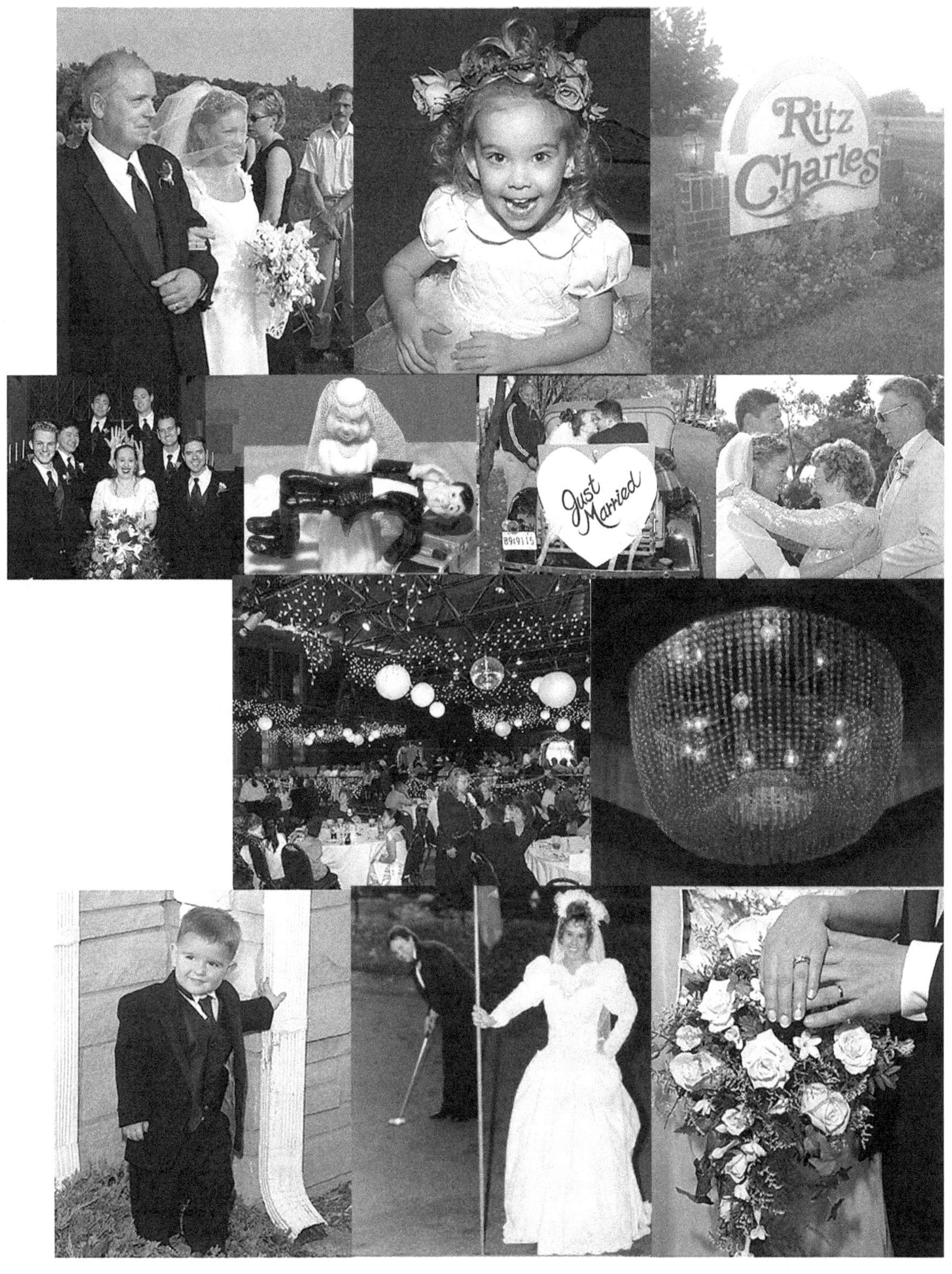
Ritz
Charles
Just
Married

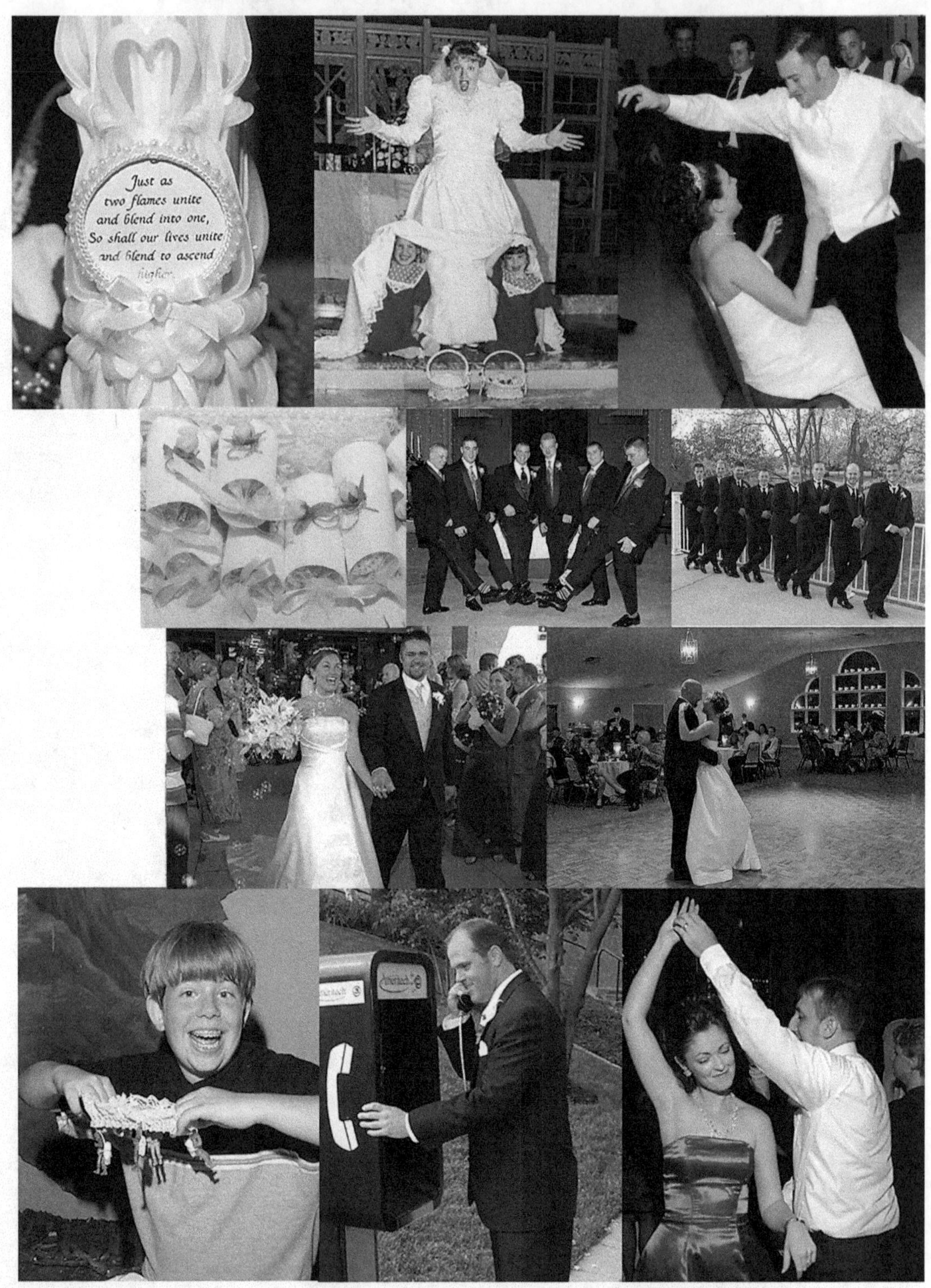
Just as
two flames unite
and blend into one,
So shall our lives unite
and blend to ascend
higher

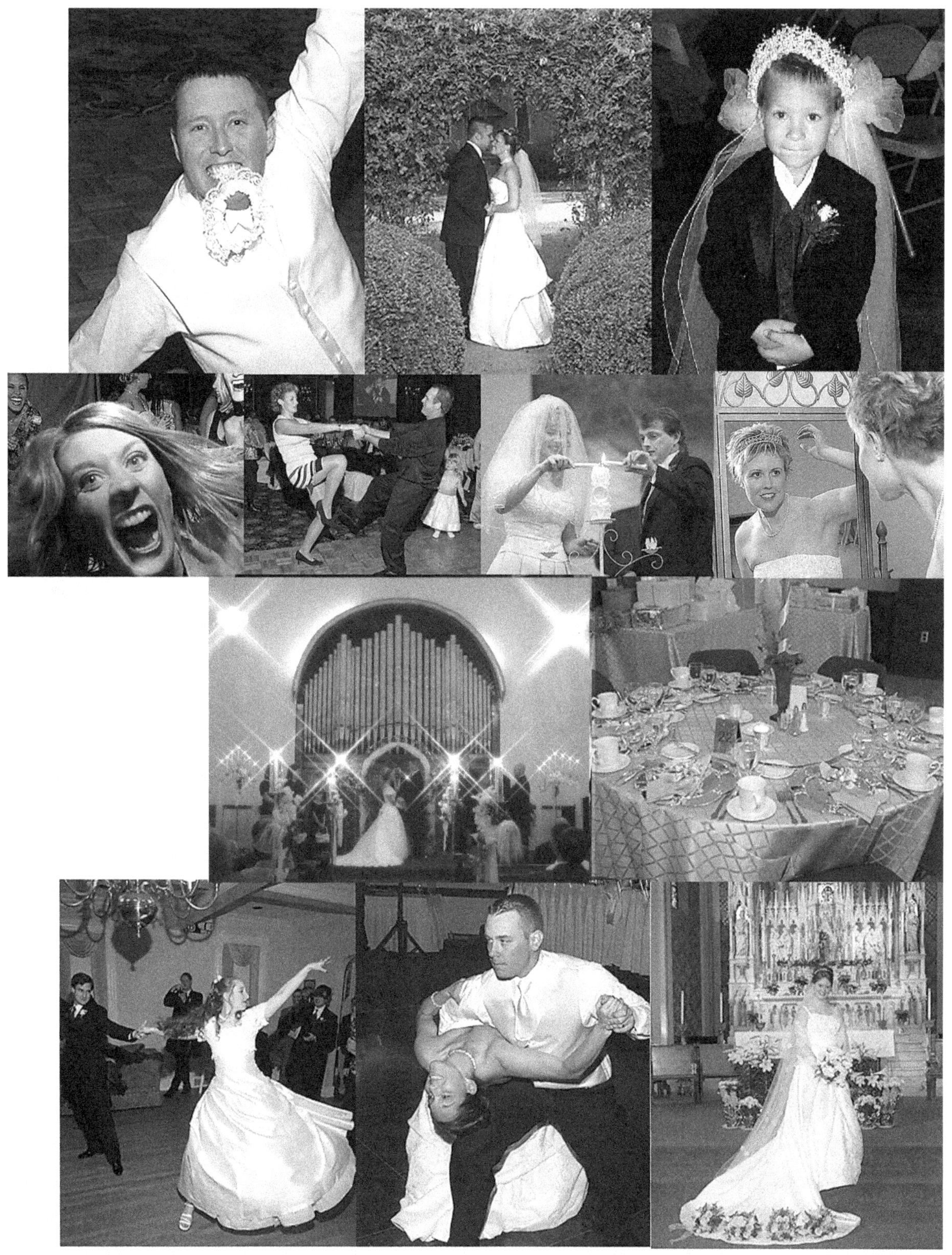

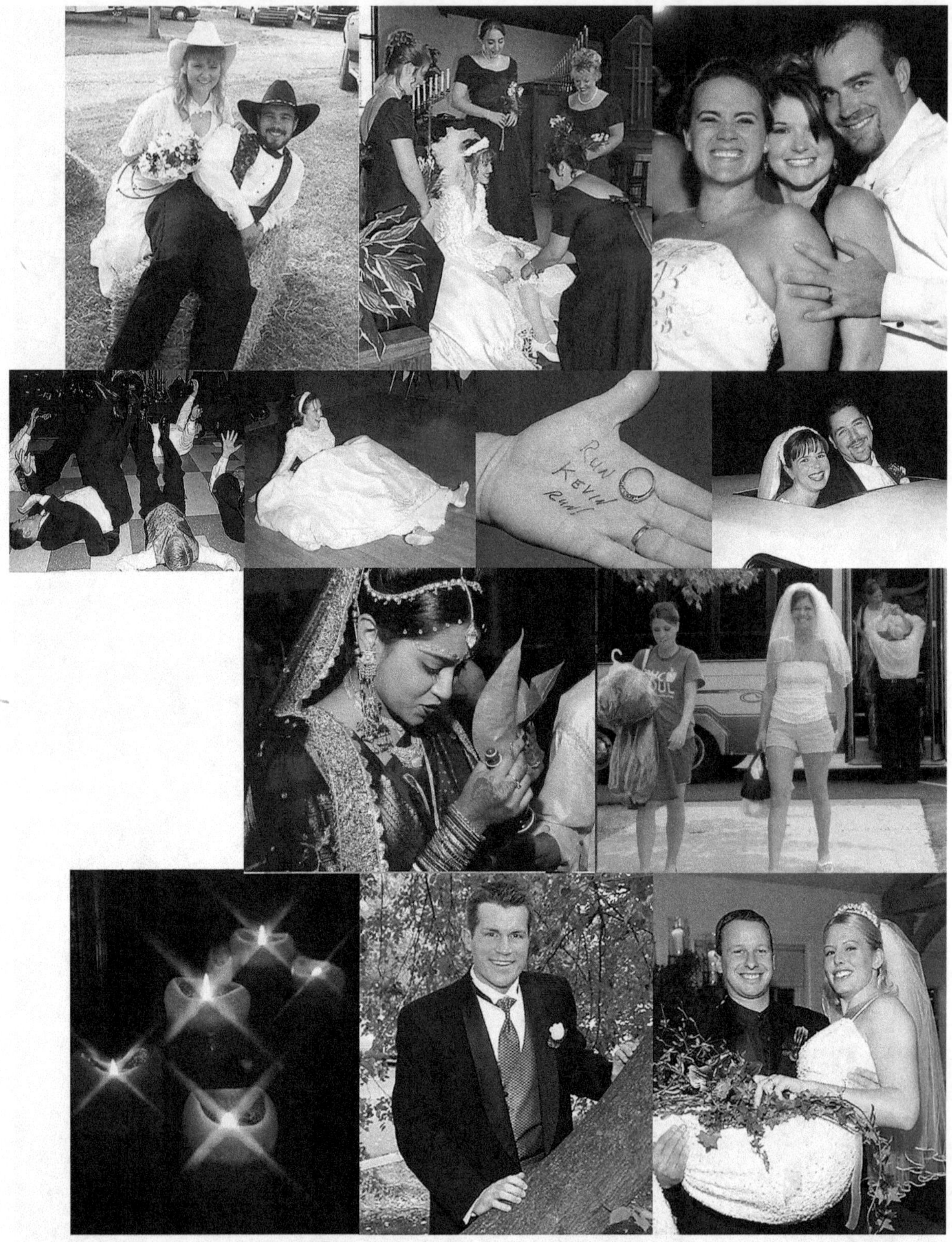
RUN
KEVIN
Run!

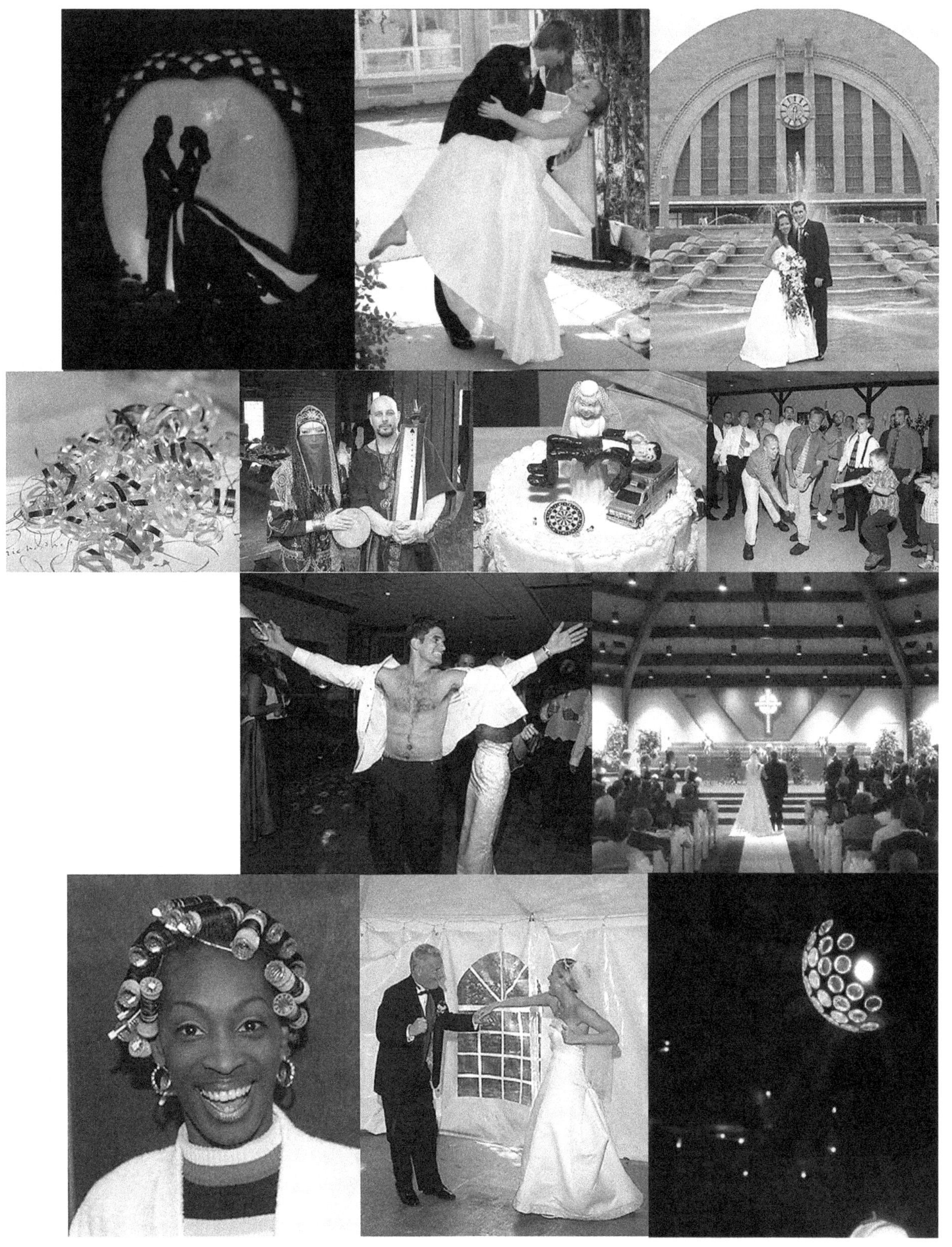

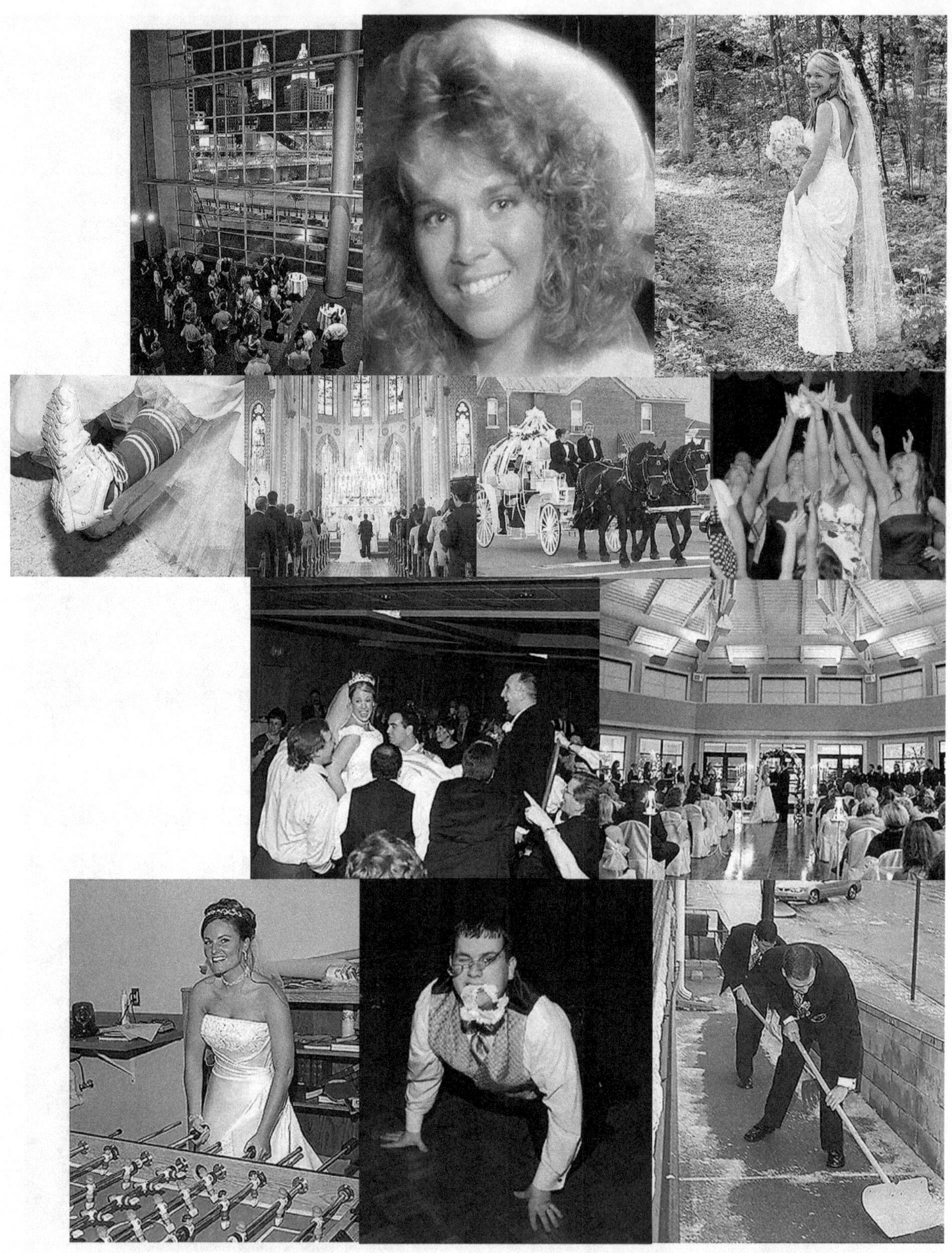

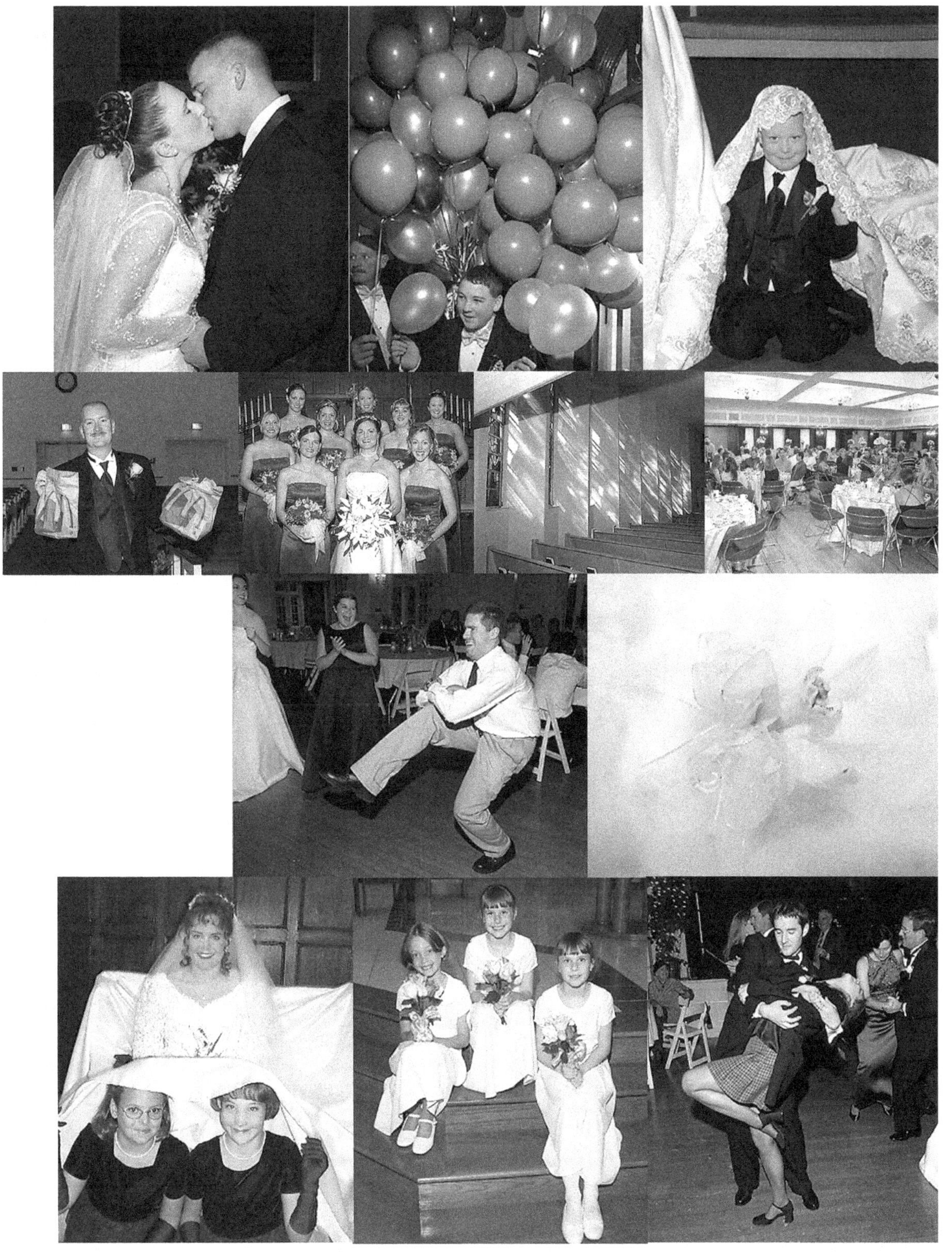

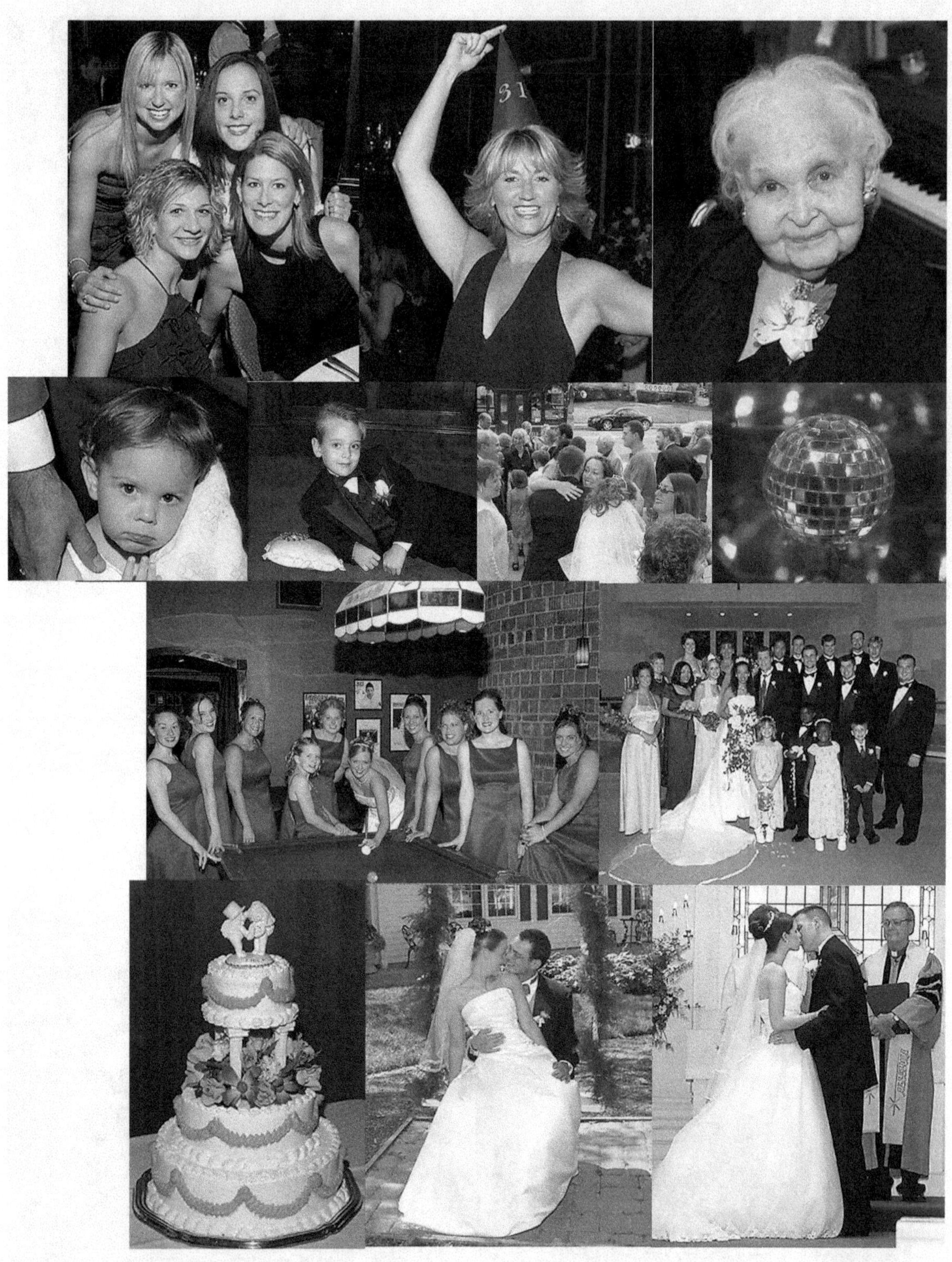

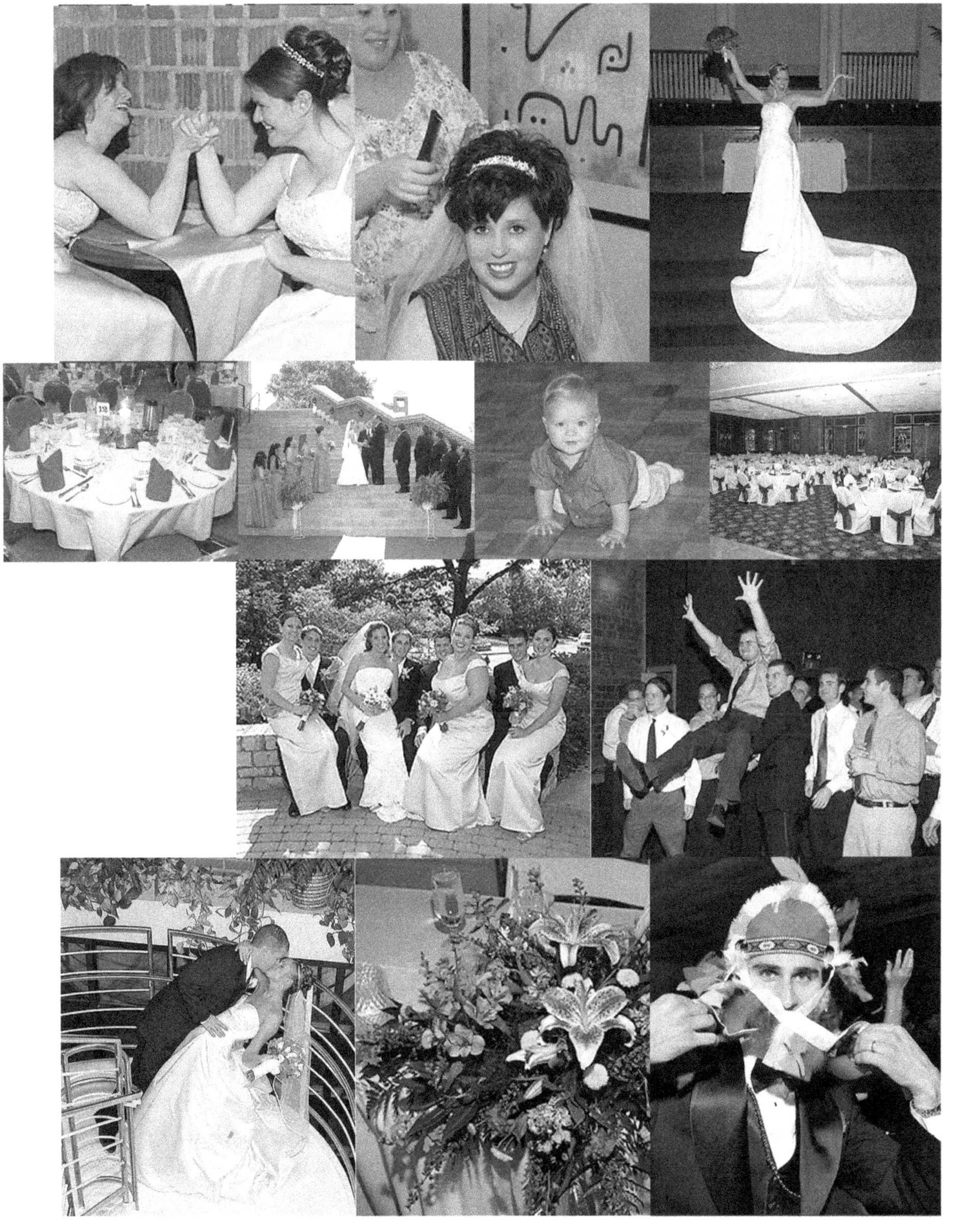

Vital Business Documents

(Each document follows, individually.)

If you are a new to wedding photography, I'm sure you don't know exactly what kinds of business documents you need to run your business effectively. I am including my vital business documents to solve that problem for you.

My **Master Wedding Post List** should be learned and committed to memory. You should know it like the back of your own hand. Using it effectively will guarantee that your coverage is as thorough as possible for your clients. If you have it thoroughly memorized, you'll never find yourself asking mentally, "***What comes next?***", especially on your formal groups involving your "cast of character photos". You will automatically know, and things will move along at lightning speed, as you work your way through your mental check list.

My emailed **Pre-Wedding, Info Gathering, Wedding Questionnaire** told me everything I would normally have gathered at a face-to-face pre-wedding consultation with the bride. It totally replaced the need, on my part, to meet with the bride before the wedding, which saved me an extra hour or two per wedding. It asked everything I would ask in person, during such a pre-wedding meeting, and gathered all the info I would gather in person.

My **Wedding Contract** was drawn up by my lawyer, at an expense of several hundred dollars. It limits my total liability to only the monies paid by the client, and keeps them from ever being able to win a law suit for any added damages under fitness for a specific purpose basis. It also required the bridal couple to get their order in for their wedding album photos within six months following their wedding date, in order to avoid having to pay a $200 late order fee. This was added after one couple brought their album print order in a full five years after their wedding, when materials to fill the order were more expensive.

The wedding contract is written as a "sale", which makes the client liable for the full balance, whether the wedding comes off on their planned wedding date or not; because I've held that date off the market just for their benefit. It also got the entire balance paid at least thirty days before the wedding. (I learned to get my money, before they went broke spending with other vendors!)

My **Email Sales Letter** turned hundreds of wedding leads into immediate sales. Those leads were gathered well in advance of their engagement announcements from the big city Bridal Guides, where I advertised as cheaply as possible, just to get those leads. During the time my advertisement ran in the Bridal Guide, I had immediate access to their huge, constantly updated online bridal database of brides who still needed my services for all open wedding dates on my schedule. For this Email, I just wrote down everything I would normally tell them during an in-person sales pitch. Having delivered it hundreds and hundreds of times in person, it was easy to put down in Email form. Man! Did it ever work! This Email is included to give you ideas as to how to make your own to use.

My **Assignment Report Card** was included in all outgoing wedding albums, along with a self-addressed stamped envelope for its return. It gathered client feedback and voluntary endorsements that I used online to advertise my services, by letting everyone know how satisfied my clients were.

Master Wedding Pose List:

Take the photos relating to the wedding you are doing.

- Outside view of church
- Individual photos of altar and aisle decorations
- Photos of the girls getting ready
  (at beauty shop, home or church)
- Photos of the guys getting dressed
- Boutonnieres being pinned on the guys' coats
- Groom with each guy in his wedding party
  (outside if possible, else at altar)
- Groom with all guys in his wedding party as a group
- Groom and ring bearer
- Groom with Mom formal
- Mom kisses groom
- Groom with Dad formal
- Both Dads with groom
- Dad shakes grooms hand
- Groom with Mom and Dad
- Groom with each set of grandparents, if present
- Each set of grandparents as couples close ups
- Groom with brothers and sisters
- Groom with his entire family
- Groom with all the girls in wedding party
- Groom being kissed by all girls in wedding party;
  have all try to kiss him
- Groom with ushers
- Full length formal of groom
- Close-up portrait of groom being relaxed
- Any other group of relatives with groom,
  who are present Aunts, Uncles, etc
- Mirror shot of bride adjusting her veil
- Bride with each girl in wedding party
  (outside if possible, else at altar)

- Bride with all girls in her wedding party as group
- Ring bearer
- Flower girl
- Ring bearer and flower girl
- Flower girl gives ring bearer kiss on cheek, if they will do it
- Bride with ring bearer and flower girl (and any junior bridesmaids)
- Bride formal full length; front and back views
- Bride's close up portrait
- Bride with her Mom close up
- Both moms with bride
- Mom looks at bride, tells her "what a beautiful bride she is" get bride's reaction
- Bride with Dad close up
- Dad gets kiss from bride close up
- Bride with Mom and Dad close up
- Bride with her brothers and sisters
- Bride with any grandparents, if present
- Bride's parents as a couple, if married
- Each set of grandparents as couples close up
- Any other group of relatives with bride, who are present Aunts, Uncles, etc
- Guest registry book
- Person manning the guest registry
- Person handing out wedding programs, as guests arrive
- Any musicians as they play
- Any readers who reads bible verses while they read
- Any singers as they sing
- Parents and all grandparents as they are come down aisle
- Mom's lighting side unity candles at altar
- Individual photos of everyone in the wedding processional as they come down aisle
- Dad kisses bride at altar

- View of ceremony without flash
  taken from real of church w/wide angle lens
- Photos of saying vows
- Groom putting ring on bride's finger
- Bride putting ring on groom's finger
- Unity candle being lit
- Priest blessing communion
- Bride taking communion
- Groom taking communion
- Wide angle of guests lined up to take communion
- Bridal kiss
- Flowers placed by bride and groom
  at feet of Virgin Mary statue
- Bride and groom giving flowers to Moms
  at end of ceremony
- Individual recessional photos of everyone
  as they come back up aisle
- Parents as they come back up the aisle
- Rice throwing as bride & groom exit church
- Receiving line photos with everyone lineup wide angle
- Guests coming through receiving line,
  featuring bride & groom receiving guests
- Each set of parents receiving guests,
  grandparents receiving guests
- Bride & groom in rear seat of getaway car,
  cheek to cheek close up
- Bride and groom with Ministers
- Bride signing marriage license
- Groom signing marriage license
- Bride and her entire extended family
- Groom and his entire extended family
- Each Dad with his brothers and sisters
- Each Dad with his parents
- Each Dad with his parents, brothers and sisters
- Each Mom with her brothers and sisters

- Each Mom with her parents
- Each Mom with her parents, brothers and sisters
- Each set of parents as a couple
- Entire wedding party with bride and groom
- Each brother with his wife and kids
- Each sister with her hubby and kids
- Any special family groups anyone requests taken
- Formal portrait of bride and groom, full length w/ train spread
- Close-up portrait of bride and groom
- Romantic as groom kisses back of bride's hand, while looking into her eyes
- Parents and wedding party photos, as each person is introduced at reception
- Photos of all decorations at reception
- DJ at work
- Everything special, unique or unusual at reception
- Any photos anyone requests taken, including posed table photos of each table of guests
- Each food item on buffet, so they can remember what they had to eat
- All important people going through buffet line
- Anyone making wedding toasts at head table, plus reaction photos
- Parents and wedding party going through buffet line
- Bride & groom first dance
- Bride dancing with her father
- Groom dancing with his mother
- Wedding party dance each couple dancing
- Parents dancing together as couples
- Grandparents dancing as couples
- Bride & groom cutting wedding cake
- Bride & groom feeding each other cake, possibly two different photos
- Bride and groom doing intertwined glasses wedding toast

- Groom removing bride's garter
- Single guys diving for bride's garter as groom flips it
- Bride ready to toss bouquet
- Guy who caught garter,
  puts it on leg of girl who caught bouquet
- Single girls diving for bouquet as bride tosses it
- Girl who caught bouquet w/ guy who caught garter
- Tons of photos of people dancing and having fun partying down
- Bride & groom leaving,
  or staged bride & groom waving bye to parents

Pre-Wedding Questionnaire: (Emailed to bride)

- Bride's Name: Occupation:
- Groom's name: Occupation:
- Wedding Date and Start Time:
- Location name and Street address of wedding:
- Location name and Street address of reception:
- Start time and ending time for reception:
- Your Phone Numbers:
- Pre-Wedding Photo start time:
- Will everyone REALLY BE READY for photos at this time? ___Yes/No? Everyone: family and grandparents really need to be there at this time.:
- Info about Bride's Family:
- How many brothers will attend wedding?
- How many with spouses &/or kids?
- How many sisters will attend wedding?
- How many with spouses &/or kids?
- How many grandparents will attend (couples or individuals?)
- Info about Groom's Family:
- How many brothers will attend wedding?
- How many with spouses & or kids?
- How many sisters will attend wedding?
- How many with spouses &/or kids?

- How many grandparents will attend
  (couples or individuals?)

- Are all the bride's & grooms parents living?

- Will all parents be attending?

- Are there any divorces/separations/remarriages
  among the parents or grandparents?
  If so, who? Does everyone get along,
  or should they be kept apart? Who?

- Number of wedding party attendants?

- Number of bridesmaids and maid/matrons of honor?

- Number of Junior bridesmaids or flower girls?

- Number of best men and groomsmen Ushers?

- Will bride and groom be facing each other
  (or their guests) during ceremony?

- How long will ceremony last?

- Will thc bridc and groom be posing together
  for photos prior to the wedding?

- Anything unusual planned during ceremony?
  (Flowers to moms or Virgin Mary, etc.)

- Who else will you want group photos of?
  (Examples: co-workers, god parents,
  high school friends, sorority sisters, etc.)

- Does bride and/or groom have children who will be attending?

- Are we doing all group photos before ceremony?

- Will you have a receiving line at wedding,
  a receiving line at reception or
  release guests a row at a time at the wedding or
  just disappear while church empties,
  then mingle with guests at reception?

- Are there church services following the wedding, which might cut us short on photo time at church? (If doing groups after ceremony, I need everyone back for photos a.s.a.p.)

- Will there be anything unusual planned at the reception? What?

Wedding Photography Agreement

Comes now Bill Collins Photography, hereinafter referred to as SELLER, and ________________________________and ____________________________________, hereinafter referred to as BUYER, and agrees as follows: That SELLER will perform professional wedding photographic services and take wedding photographs at the request of BUYER at __________ on _______ _____/_____/____ at the following wedding location: ____, which is located at ________________ and at the reception, which is to be held at __________________________________, which is located at: ____. SELLER agrees to sell to BUYER said services and the following wedding photo package from SELLER'S Wedding Package Price List: ______________________________ for the price of $________ plus 7% sales tax and BUYER agrees to purchase said package at said price. A $600.00 non-refundable retainer locks BUYER'S wedding date on SELLER'S schedule, with full balance due to be paid at least 30 days prior to the scheduled wedding date. Full balance is due at that time, even in the event of a cancellation or postponement of the wedding ceremony, since SELLER has relinquished, from the time of agreement signing, the opportunity to be available to all other possible clients for that date and time.

It is understood and agreed to by BUYER and SELLER that under any and all circumstances and conditions the SELLER'S liability shall not exceed the refund of any monies paid to SELLER by BUYER, minus any non-refundable retainers that BUYER has paid to SELLER to secure SELLER'S services. SELLER disclaims the implied warranties of merchantability and fitness for a particular purpose for all photographs, whether in color or in black and white.

Acting as agent for all who appear in the BUYER'S wedding photographs, BUYER grants SELLER the rights to use said images as samples, for display and to publish and enter said images into photo print competitions and for any advertising purposes and for any other purposes SELLER sees fit.

It is further agreed by SELLER and BUYER that the price of the wedding photo package BUYER purchases from SELLER is based on SELLER being able to fill BUYER'S purchased wedding photo package order WITHIN SIX MONTHS of they BUYER'S wedding date. **Time being of the essence, BUYER therefore agrees to furnish SELLER with a complete written list of BUYER'S selections for BUYER'S purchased wedding photo package order within six months following BUYER'S wedding date.**

BUYER also agrees to pay SELLER a two hundred dollar ($200) late order fee, should BUYER'S selection list for said package order fail to reach the SELLER within six months following BUYER'S wedding date. SELLER is in no way obligated to deliver any finished photographs from BUYER'S wedding to BUYER, until after the two hundred late order fee has been paid to SELLER when six months following the BUYER'S wedding date has passed without SELLER receiving said package photo selection list.

Any provision of this agreement prohibited by the laws of any State, shall, as to such State, be ineffective to the extent of such prohibition without invalidating the remaining portions of this Wedding Photography Agreement.

No modification of any of the terms or conditions hereof shall be valid in any event, and the BUYER expressly waives the right to rely thereon, unless made in writing and duly executed by the SELLER. BUYER has read this agreement and acknowledges receipt of a copy of same. Signing by BUYER and by SELLER are in substitution and in completion of the original.

______________________, ___/___/____

(" SELLER") ("DATE")

______________________, ___/___/____

("BUYER") ("DATE")

______________________, ___/___/____

("BUYER) ("DATE)

Notice how this agreement: (1) limits your liability to just the monies the client has paid you. (2) forces bridal couples to order their album prints within six months of the wedding, in order to avoid a $200 late order fee. (This keeps them from turning in their album order five years following the wedding! It happened to me!)

Top Ten Reasons Why You'll Want ProWeddingPhotos As Your Wedding Photographer!

The following is the sales-making email I sent out to all prospects telling what set me apart from all the other photographers they could hire:

I'm replying to your RESERVATION request you made for your wedding date from either my wedding photography website, proweddingphotos.com or from the area's Bridal Guide.

If you are just requesting info, this email should do the job.

He's Proposed: Now allow me! (I'm unique!)

1.) Brides in Indy/Cincy/Dayton and Columbus, OH area are constantly telling me I offer twice as much for half the price of big city wedding photographers in my half dozen or so wedding photo package offers. That's why I'm able to advertise as having, "America's Best Value Wedding Photography Packages!"

Photographers use price to control how many weddings they "have to do" each year, especially those photographers who hate doing weddings. They want to make max profit per wedding, so they don't have to do very many per year!

Since I enjoy doing weddings so much, I keep my prices low, in order to "get to do" as many weddings as possible. (I did 47 in '03.) I could easily raise my prices and make as much per year while doing fewer weddings to earn it, but I enjoy the experience so much I keep my package prices down in order to get to do as many as I can during the year..

2.) Totally digital top notch professional quality coverage is available. You'll actually get to see all your wedding photos while enjoying your reception meal in the form of a slideshow on my laptop computer! Your relatives and guests will get to enjoy this slideshow once you start dancing and partying!

600 to 1,000+ exposures is my typical coverage on the average wedding, with usually three or more exposures are taken of every important group photo for you to select from.

You'll find, too, in the photos I print for your albums and print orders, those prints are fully retouched, no blemishes, no bags under anyone's eyes, no shine on cheeks, chins or foreheads, etc. Everyone looks their best. Most wedding photographers will usually take one or two photos of the wedding toasts, while it's typical for me to get maybe a dozen or more during the toasts! (The same is true with all the important happenings at your wedding/reception! I'm like the Energizer Bunny. I just keep on shooting!)

3.) On your wedding coverage, you'll find I'm very laid back and flexible. I tend to "go with the flow, lay on my back and float downstream", getting what photos I can, when I can. Then later adding in any photos which didn't get taken as planned, due to any important people arriving late, etc.! (It's murder to try to "swim upstream or try to control the flow of a wedding! That's the one thing I try to avoid doing.")

With 40 years of wedding photo experience, (I started when I was only 18 years old; so I'm not old and I still run marathons!) the last 16 years of which have been as a full time professional wedding photographer/studio owner, I can photograph your wedding how ever it ends up coming off...with the absolute least amount of interruption and slowing down the festivities of the day!

4.) I don't charge any mileage charges on weddings within my Indy/Cincy/Dayton, OH coverage area and never charge any shipping charges on mailing out your album of photos! I think you'll find I am more able and willing to give you much better individual service than "local, big city studio" are willing to give you.

5.) Any guest at your wedding, absolutely ANYONE, can request group photos they would like taken and I'll happily take two or three photos of each of their groups for them. (I have always viewed my job description as "people pleaser" whenever possible! I enjoy saying "yes" to all requests for photos!)

I thoroughly enjoy doing weddings and probably have as much fun capturing your memories, festivities and good times for you as anyone has who attends your wedding/reception! And it ends up showing in everything I do at your wedding and reception.

It's not at all unusual for guests to come up to me, when they see me packing my gear at the end of my coverage, just to tell me how amazed and impressed they are with how thoroughly I've covered the festivities and how much they enjoyed my laptop slideshow of the wedding and reception photos!

6.) The really good news is if I sent you this email, it means I am, at least at the time I sent the email, available to photograph your wedding for you on your selected wedding date. I am, however, a one photographer studio and as such, dates don't stay available very long. The bad news is I probably also emailed this to at least a half dozen to a dozen other brides who share your wedding date when I emailed you. (I was booked 30 weddings into 2004, before the year even began.)

7). If you are getting married in the "off-season", you can take advantage of my special offer which allows you to add an additional 12 8x10's to the photo package of your choice for only an additional $39.00! What a bargain! ("Off-season" is defined in my wedding price list/literature package, which you can receive simply by responding to this email, requesting it.)

8.) I'm almost always the very first to arrive at the wedding site on the wedding date. Usually the church isn't even unlocked yet when I first arrive. I always bring at least twice the equipment I will need to do the assignment, as back up equipment in case any of my equipments suddenly quits working.

I've pioneered digital wedding photography in this area of the country and have photographers calling me every week or so, wanting to pick my brain about their "going digital" and wanting to know if they can "get by" buying and using a $1,000 pro-sumer digital camera for weddings! Yikes!

My two Nikon D1x pro digital cameras run about $5,000 each just for each camera body and I use two of them on the wedding day! Not to mention the four different high quality Nikon (expensive, up to $1,800 each) lenses I bring and the three Nikon computerized flash units ($400 each). The point I'm making here is I NEVER try to "get by" or use pro-sumer grade equipment! Nothing but the very best for me, when it comes to equipment to do my wedding assignments! And I bring plenty of backup equipment to assure I'll always be able to complete the assignment as planned.

9.) You can visit my huge web site and see online sample photos, complete sets of weddings online (600 to over 1,000+ photos each), complete wedding photo package info and prices, advice, fun stuff and more at: ProWeddingPhotos.com.

10.) Upon request, I can give references on lots of weddings in your area I've photographed within the last couple of years. Any of the brides who's wedding I've done will be happy to tell you just how fortunate you'll be to be able to have me photograph your wedding!

After photographing weddings for 40 years and being trained by better about a dozen of the world's top Master Wedding Photographers in workshops and seminars over the years and studying at Winona International School of Professional Photography, which is run by the Professional Photographers of America, I've blended the very best of everything I've learned into my own special style which mixes the needed traditional group photo taking...in a 20 to 30 minute session, with a free form photojournalistic style during the rest of the day to capture everything happening at your wedding in a smooth flow as it happens.

Unlike a lot of studios who insist on telling you that they are "specialists" in whatever kind of photography you need done, I am indeed a true wedding photography specialist. My practice is so specialized that well over 98 percent of my total annual income is derived solely from wedding photography, mostly in Indy, Cincy and Dayton, OH.

Did you know about a fourth of the studio photographers who do weddings, have come to absolutely hate doing weddings...and only do them because they need the income weddings generate to keep their studios going? They'll never tell you this or even hint at it during the hiring process....but it usually seems to rear its ugly head once they actually get on the job! Pity the bride who gets hold of a wedding hating photographer!

How's my service when it comes to filling your album print order? A lot of times, when I am caught up when an order comes in the mail first thing in the morning, I am able to spend the day producing the order, getting the album ready and turn it around in the mail late in the same afternoon it was received! Now that's service!

I hope we can both benefit greatly by having me photograph your wedding for you!

My Main Wedding Page: http://www.ProWeddingPhotos.com/index.htm?email

Thanks, Bill Collins Wedding Photography

Photographer's Wedding Assignment Report Card:

(***Enclosed in finished wedding albums with SASE.***)

Bride's Name: Groom's Name:

Wedding date and Location:

On a scale of 1 to 10, with one being "terrible" and ten being "best imaginable", please rate the following questions about your experience with me:

1. How thorough did you find my coverage?

2. Did I miss taking any photos you wanted taken at your wedding? (Y/N)

(If yes, please elaborate on back of report card.)

3. How easy was I to get along with?

4. How thoroughly did I satisfy you on your wedding day?

5. How much do you like your finished photos?

6. Is there anything I could have done to please you more? (Y/N)

(If yes, please elaborate on back of report card.)

7. How likely would you be to recommend me to others?

8. How much did I help to get people to relax during the group photos?

9. How quickly did I move people through during group photos?

10. Is there anything I could have done, but didn't, to make your day better? (Y/N)

(If yes, elaborate on back of report card.)

11. Is there anything I did that pleasingly surprised you? (Y/N)

(If yes, please elaborate on back of report card.)

12. How much value did you find my package contained for you?

13. How reasonable did you find my prices?

COMMENTS: (feel free to continue on back of report card.)

May quote you in my advertising and elsewhere? Please indicate "Yes" by signing the line below:

Yes, you may quote me: Signed: ______________________________ Date:_______

Chapter 1: You Probably Don't Know

How to Improve Quickly at Wedding Photography

I presume you purchased this book because you want to be a better professional wedding photographer. I am at the other end of that spectrum, being semi-retired after a 45-year career as a wedding photographer in the Midwest regional markets, serving the Indianapolis, Cincinnati, and Dayton, Ohio areas. I have a lifetime of knowledge, learning, and experiences to share with you.

From my unique vantage point, there really doesn't seem to be much that people need to learn to become a good wedding photographer. I want to help guide you in your learning, so you go down the most easily traversed, straight road towards knowing what you are doing, while helping you avoid all those dangerous steep learning curves along the way.

Now, by this point you have to be asking yourself, 'Is this guy full of himself?' Not at all. I lost any inflated ego I might have had after just a few years in the business, and settled down to simply concentrating on giving each of my clients the best wedding coverage I could. I always thought of myself just a well-trained and experienced craftsman plying his trade, rather than some kind of artsy-fartsy artist; the latter type of photographer usually fails miserably at keeping their ego in check. My attitude was: get the job done, do it right, make it flow, and move on.

I have noticed that a lot of photographers online seem to really concentrate on learning post-production photo tweaking (Photoshop), instead of learning how to take good straight-out-of-the-camera photos that need only minimal tweaking. They also seem to rely heavily upon getting critiques of their photos from other online photographers, who, for the most part, don't seem to be much further advanced than they are. In this kind of learning environment, the learning process is bound to be painfully slow and the learning curve a lot steeper than it needs to be.

After a couple of decades of slow-learning years from being self-taught, I really learned photography back during the 1980s and 1990s, by going to the Professional Photography Association's Winona International School of Professional Photography. There I received in-person instruction from several of the best PPA Master Photographers in the country, with them being able to instantly correct me when I made mistakes while learning. They probably taught their students more, during each of their three-to-five-day-long, knowledge-packed courses on a given subject at Winona, than you would learn by taking an entire semester at other photography schools. On your own, it would likely take you years to learn what they managed to teach in just a few short days. Everything at Winona is taught with the idea that you can go straight home to your photography studio and use the skills you just learned to immediately begin earning your living.

Looking at it now, from the other side of the fence, there isn't that much you need to learn to quickly put yourself on solid footing as a good professional wedding photographer. My desire is to steer you, in your learning, down an easily traversed, straight road towards excellence in what you do, so you can avoid all those steep and dangerous learning curves.

To quickly become an excellent wedding photographer, you should concentrate on learning how to:

- Use the manual exposure mode on your camera to always get good exposure levels in your photos, without under-exposing or over-exposing your subjects or their backgrounds. In sunny outdoor settings, you want to learn how to make the lighting on your main foreground subjects match the lighting levels of the background, so they will look naturally lit, without the photo looking like you had used flash.

  .

  When using fill flash, remember that your camera's shutter speed controls the level of background lighting that passes through your lens, while the aperture setting on your camera controls the strength of your fill flash lighting. Experiment mixing those two lighting sources to get realistic, natural-looking, and pleasing results.
- Properly frame up your images so that your "money-shot" nearly fills your viewfinder before taking the photo. If you are not comfortable moving in really close to your subjects to do that, then use the zoom feature on your camera lens to move your camera's vantage point in close to your subjects, without invading their personal space. Nailing your money-shot really elevates the level of your work, and will help convince knowledgeable people that you have really learned your craft.
- Frame up your subject as a vertical, when photographing just one or two people, and unlearn photographing them as landscape-oriented portraits. In my humble opinion, taking landscape-oriented portraits makes your work look like a beginner's. I visit this topic again in more detail in Chapter 3.
- Use good portrait-posing techniques, including how to attractively pose hands and feet and how to turn your static poses into something more dynamic. Get people to relax and become comfortable.
- Pose groups of people to make them compact, balanced, and attractive, building groups vertically, instead of horizontally. Work quickly and efficiently, and keep all your people at hand for groups, while photographing them, so you don't spend time trying to round them up for each group photo.
- Get the job done using minimal amounts of equipment by traveling as lightly-loaded as possible, while on location. Carrying more equipment usually just makes your job harder as the day wears on. I know I was amazed when Donald Jack, top Master Photographer, showed us students just how little equipment he took with him to do his weddings.
- Market yourself and get yourself hired for all the weddings you want to photograph. You'll get to see what worked for me, and what didn't.
- Properly use multiple lighting on formal portraits. Once you know how to take good portraits with multiple light sources, you can apply this knowledge to weddings by using off-camera flash setups. All those multiple off-camera flash setups photographers use at weddings are just portrait lighting techniques that have been put into use on location. Portrait lighting is all about controlling where the shadows fall on the face in order to make your subject look three-dimensional, and possibly thinner, in their photos.

  .

  Multiple lighting is easier to learn and control in a studio environment, where you use modeling lights to be able to see where the shadows fall on your subjects' faces. (After learning and using multiple off-camera lighting on location for a few years, I finally switched to using a single elevated and diffused on-camera flash, which cut the amount of equipment I had to lug around by about two-thirds. I revisit this subject again later in this book, giving even more reasons for that decision.) This is a subject you might want to put on the back burner, to study after you master everything else you need to know. The better you are when you tackle this subject, the easier it will be to learn.

If you were to sign up at Winona for a basic portraiture course, followed immediately by advanced portraiture and a wedding photography courses, you could have most of the knowledge you need to know under your belt in just a couple of weeks' worth of study. That is how quickly and thoroughly they teach you there. Agreed, it is going to cost you some money to take those courses, but I think that beats plodding along for several years trying to learn it on your own.

When I wrote this book, I reached into my memory to remember exactly how they taught me everything I learned at Winona and put it down to share with my readers, so you all would not have to spend as much money as I did to learn the same techniques. I also put down what I learned and encountered over my 45-year career as a wedding photographer. I liken you reading my book to you gaining 45 years of experience in one short, easy, and possibly even fun read.

Chapter 2: Posing Groups Like a Pro

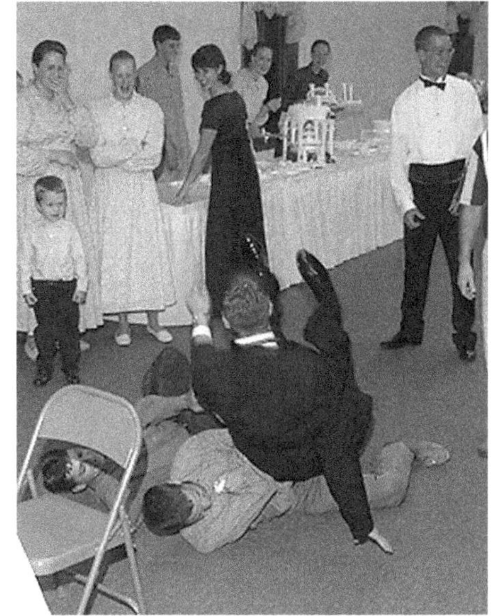

In the photo at the right, three guys are all diving for the bride's garter. The guy in the lightest colored shirt has the garter clutched to his chest. The guy in the dark suit is in the process of sailing over the top of the other two in midair. This is another example of nailing peak action in your photos.

If I ever saw the bride take her veil off and lay it aside at the reception, I would ask her if I could borrow it for a photo. Then I would track down the groom, put the bride's veil on him and get him to ham it up for a couple of photos of him wearing the veil! That always made for fun photos!

There were a couple of other fun shots I liked to do when the situation was right. If I saw three guys or girls from the wedding party standing around together, I would line them up next to each other and tell the first one, "cover your eyes"; the second one, "cover your ears"; and the third one, "cover your mouth." Snap. I had the perfect "See no evil, hear no evil, speak no evil" monkey photo. They were usually smart enough to see what I was doing by the time the photo was taken. If not, they usually got the joke as soon as I showed them the photo after taking it.

With a larger group, I might tell them all to make circles with their thumbs and index fingers and put them up to their eyes, so it looked like they were wearing goofy glasses or looking through binoculars.

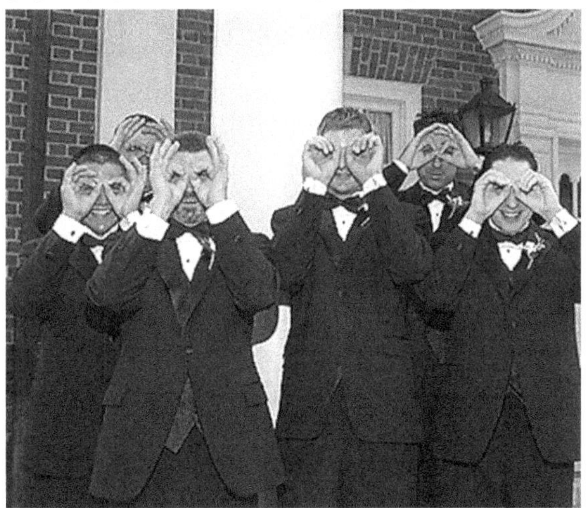

I know what it feels like to be a part of this pose. My teacher at Winona School of Professional Photography made us all do that pose in a class photo. It was also the one she picked for us to bring home as our 8x10 graduating class photo.

Sometimes, I took several exposures within a second or two, by using my camera's continuous exposure mode and keeping the shutter depressed during peak action. When I did, I might get a few slightly underexposed images by shooting faster than my flash unit could recycle its charge. I'd correct the underexposure on these images in Adobe Lightroom before burning the bride's CDs.

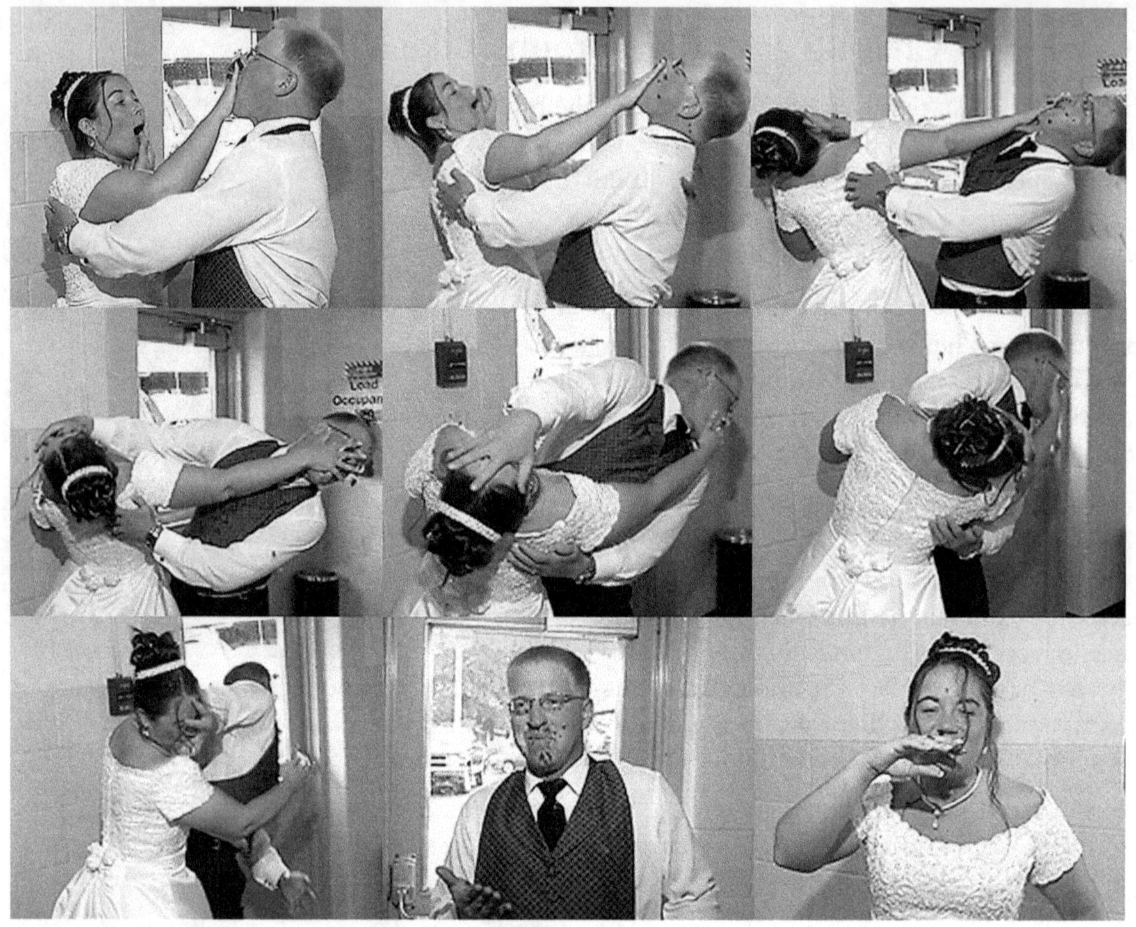

Example of multiple exposures, taken faster than my flash unit could keep up, after images were corrected for under exposures. These nine were taken in about three seconds time. Is that capturing all the peak action, or what?

When I was in my forties, I made a point of learning how to take some really super difficult to do and neat-looking Hollywood movie style in-camera matte box double exposures. See the one below. They were in vogue back then, but aren't done nearly as commonly now. The movie industry created these matte box double exposure type special effects for their movies.

If you want to know step-by-step how to take these complicated matte box double exposures, email me at, proweddingphotos at yahoo dot com. I'll send you a thousand word description I wrote of how it is done. When using film cameras, you only got one chance per wedding to get it right.

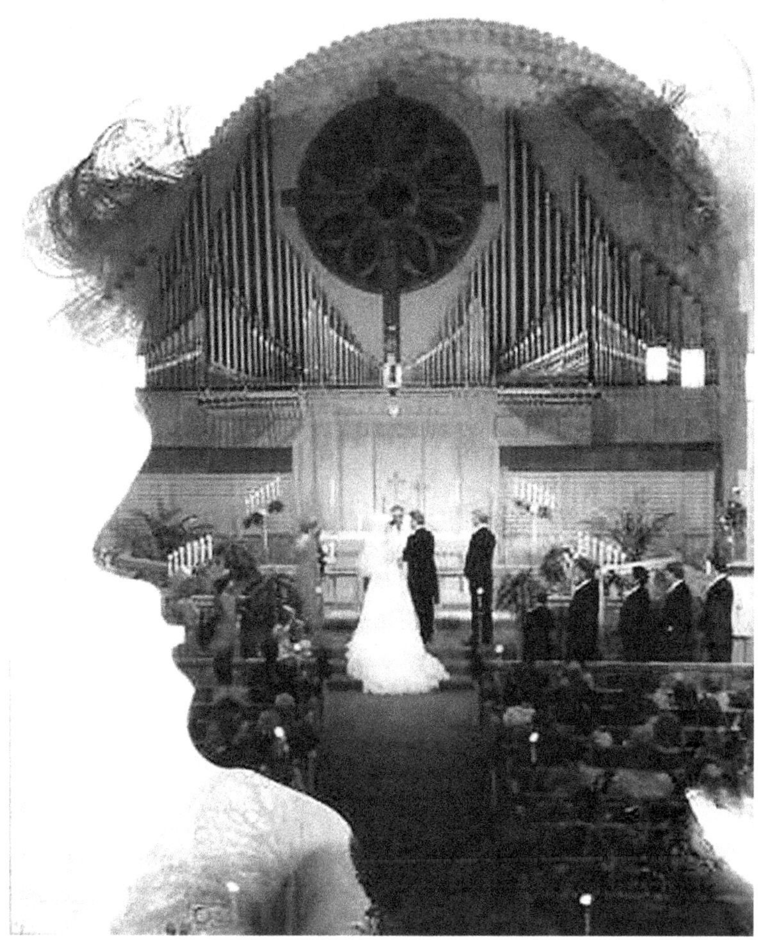

Matte Box in-camera double exposure of bride thinking about her wedding.

Guys, especially in wedding party photos, tend to naturally clasp one hand over the other, covering their groin area during photos, probably because they don't know what else to do with their hands for the photo and they are nervous. This is called the "fig leaf pose". We were taught it was to be avoided, as it sure doesn't look good, or professional, in photos.

One of the most difficult jobs to do at a reception is when the bride, or her mom, asked you to take "table shots" of everyone sitting at each table throughout the entire reception hall. Usually, you only have the meal time to take these photos. People are constantly coming and going from these tables during the meal; whether they're just milling around, going to the restroom, going outside to smoke, or going through the buffet. It was very difficult to keep track of which tables I had done and which ones I had skipped because of the table being half-empty when I got to it, making it one I'd have to make a mental note to do later, when the table was full again.

Finally, I learned to draw out a seating chart of the tables on a piece of paper and mark each table off, as its photo was taken. Marking the tables, as I did them, made it easy for me not to miss photographing any tables.

In order to get the best table groupings, I would have the guests nearest the camera move around the table and stand behind those seated on the opposite side of the table.

I was always glad to get the table shots completed. Requests for table shots usually meant that I wouldn't have time to eat supper myself. By the time I was done doing table shots, suppertime was over and it was time for me to start photographing all the festivities.

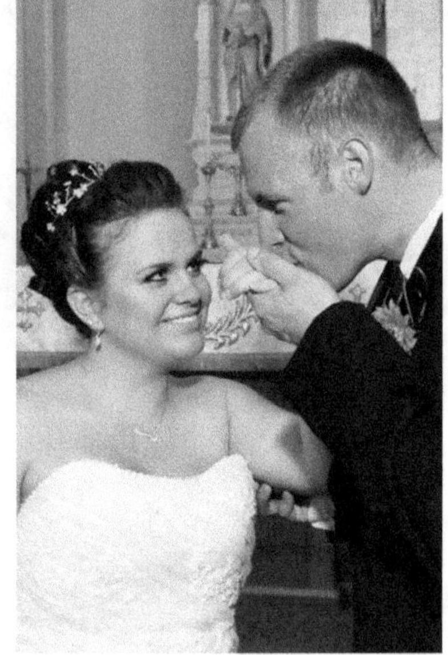

Here are instructions for how to take one of my favorite posed romantic shots of the bride and groom, so you can understand how it is done. Have the couple face each other while standing close to each other. Tell the groom to take the bride's hand in his hand and to look directly into her eyes.

Once you have them in your viewfinder and are ready to snap the photo, direct the groom by saying, "Keep eye contact, don't break it. Bring her hand up and kiss the back of her hand." When he has done so, snap your photo, capturing the bride's immediate smile and pleased reaction to the groom's romantic gesture.

There is a close-up pose of the bridal couple, that I came up with from my portrait training days, which might need explanation. It's usually done at the front of the church. The bride lays on her side, with her hip and elbow on the floor and her bridal flowers in her hands in front of her body. The groom gets down on his side, right behind the bride, with his feet facing in the opposite direction. They are "crossed over" each other a bit, making an "X". This is done by placing the groom to overlap his bride slightly. He is on one hip, with one totally outstretched stiff arm, elbow locked, with the palm of his hand on the floor, holding him up. When they are both on the same floor level, this puts his head about a head's height higher than hers.

The couple, when viewed from head on, are cheek-to-cheek close. Move in and take this as a tightly framed vertically-oriented photograph, showing them from about the hips up.

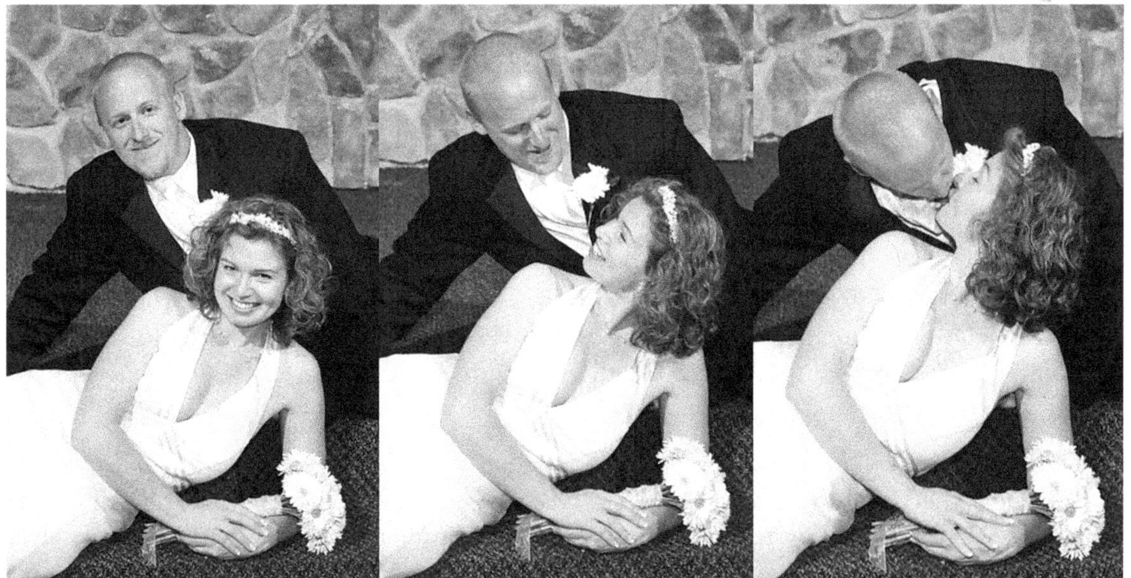

First photo: cheek-to-cheek, smiling at the camera. Second photo: immediately have the couple turn their heads so they are gazing into each other's eyes. Third photo: have them kiss. Here the bride and groom are on different levels, as she is down one step's height from the groom.

This pose sequence produces a really quick three-pose series that is tremendously popular. It is well worth the effort it takes to set it up. Before taking it, though, I always ask the bride and groom if they mind working just a little bit for a really good photo. I tell them it involves them getting down on the floor. If they are game, off we go with the posing. If they say no, then it is on to something else.

What do you do when, for example, the bride's parents are the life of the party during the reception and you get tons of photos showing them dancing and having a good time; but the groom's parents never get out on the dance floor and are quite demure, just staying seated, never giving you any good photo opportunities of them enjoying the festivities during the evening?

I had this frustrating phenomenon happen to me twice, and after one of those weddings, the bride complained about the unbalanced coverage I had of the bride's and groom's parents: plenty of photos of one set and few of the other. All I could do was explain how one set of parents had made themselves more available for photos than the other set of parents did. Lesson Learned: If you see this happening, then I would recommend trying to get some photos of the more low-key parents, even if it is just of them talking to other guests at their table! Do it in self-defense!

Few churches will allow you to photograph the ceremony using flash. To get around this, I would always use a super-fast, long zoom lens on one camera, mounted on a professional grade tripod for steadiness. I usually took photos of the ceremony with the lens wide open at f/2.8, using a slow shutter speed of 1/30 of a second or so in the low light.

I always used the fastest shutter speed I could, 1/60 of a second when possible, to get rid of the possibility of images being blurred by the subjects' movements. People don't move particularly quickly during wedding ceremonies, but you can still end up with blurred images, if you go down to 1/15 of a second or slower.

With digital, I was able to bump the ISO (film speed) up to 1600 (now, with better cameras, photographers think nothing of shooting up to 6400 ISO) to simulate shooting with fast film that is really made for use in low light photography. We didn't even have ISO 1600 speed film available in the day I shot film! ISO 400 was considered fast film back then. It pretty much sucked in low light, too.

That combination of a super-fast low-light lens, tripod mounted, using large aperture, and fast ISO film speed setting did a super job of creating great photos in low existing light during the ceremony.

A long Nikon or Cannon pro-level zoom lens with those kinds of capabilities cost around $1,750 in 1998, so it isn't cheap. Sometimes you just can't get by with cheap, when you want good quality. I always felt my clients deserved to have me use the very best equipment available to capture their images.

Lately, I've noticed prices on all digital camera equipment have dropped significantly. I see Nikon camera kits everywhere now at about $495 or less, featuring bodies which are probably better than what I paid $4,995 for when I first started purchasing digital camera bodies. Good lenses are always going to cost a lot more than the lenses they put in these low-priced kits nowadays. They are a really good investment, too.

I always kept my second camera within arm's reach, set up and ready to take flash photos. Just as soon as I captured the final bridal kiss at the altar with the long lens, I immediately picked up my other camera and was ready, in just a second, to catch the couple coming back up the aisle.

It made me feel rushed when I had to switch over to flash photography using just one camera rig. I had to change so many camera settings (ISO, aperture, white balance, and shutter speed) and get the flash turned on again, all in only about three seconds, because the bride and groom would now be coming back up the aisle towards me at a fast clip, and you know this is not a photo opportunity to be missed.

I used to take rear views of the ceremony from the church balcony, but I found it put me too far out of position to feel comfortable. I finally decided to photograph everything from floor level. There really isn't enough difference in the photos produced from the two different locations to make it worth the added pressure of possibly getting caught out of position at a critical time, or even risk missing getting to photograph a part of the ceremony, while I was en route to the balcony and back down again.

A lot of those old church steps to the balcony were squeaky and noisy, too, so I created a disturbance when I went up and down them during the ceremony. I never liked that. Photographing everything from ground level simplified life for me, and I never regretted making my decision.

By the way, get rid of the word "shoot" from your vocabulary. Amateurs shoot pictures. Pros take photographs and create masterpieces. It is not nice to shoot people, either. They will put you in jail for shooting people. Shooting someone could even prove fatal.

Posing trade secrets worth killing for:

My teachers at Winona School of Professional Photography always told their students, "You have to go home and put this knowledge to use right away, if you want to retain it. It is taught and learned solely on a 'use it or lose it' basis."

They would use a model, set a pose, improve it by just one tiny step, then let each student look through their camera's eyepiece to see just how much each tiny step of refinement improved the end product. Getting to see the progression of those tiny steps is what really drove home just how important each tiny refining tweak was towards producing the end product

The teachers would go through this drill over and over, through each and every tiny step of refined improvement they added before taking the finished photo. That's why I'm going to tell you how to pose people in tiny steps, too. I just wish we had a camera set up so you could look through the eyepiece and see how each tiny refinement contributes to the final product.

I'm going to do my best to teach you how I was taught by Master Photographers to take a good half-length female studio portrait. Almost all of what I teach in this chapter can be adapted for professional use in doing weddings, too.

Seat the subject so she is facing about a third of the way sideways (about 30 degrees from being head-on to the camera) and displaying good posture. This slims her down a bit. Head-on seating shows her at their broadest.

If she isn't displaying good posture and are slumped over a bit, just place your thumb in the small of her back and the tips of your fingers on her shoulder. Pull back slightly with your fingers, while pushing in lightly with your thumb in the small of her back. You'll find this snaps her into a sitting position with excellent posture, and it works every time! Most people slump and don't even realize it.

You might want to let her know what you'll be doing before straightening her posture, so as not to surprise her. You don't want to have her thinking you are trying to get fresh with her.

Place her hands so they look aesthetically pleasing, possibly with her hands overlapping or with only one hand showing. You also want to make sure to photograph her hands so you are seeing the thin bottom blade of her hand, with the fingers slightly curled and the thumb touching her first finger.

Posing her hands in this way prevents having her hands look like big fat meat cleavers in the photos. You are now seeing the thin bottom edge view of her hand, not the big fleshy back of her hands. Hand posing is an art unto itself.

Next, you might even want to "break her wrist" a little bit by having her pull her partially closed hand up slightly, towards her elbow. This lowers the wrist slightly and breaks the straight line of the extended forearm and makes it look much more relaxed and natural in the photographs.

Next, have her turn her head away from the camera by about 20 to 30 degrees. This is referred to as a 2/3's facial view, which is said to be the most flattering angle you can use to photograph a face.

Her eyes are now directed to look back into the camera lens, without her turning her head. Her head is next tilted sideways just slightly out of vertical alignment to add tons of attitude and personality to the photo. Her chin is lowered ever so slightly for even more attitude.

You have created the upper half of what photographers call the feminine "S" curve, which is very flattering when photographing women. In full-length poses, you can achieve the full S-curve effect for even greater impact. In Chapter 6, I'll describe how to pose women's legs and feet to give them a clothing model pose.

You can now choose to tilt (rotate) your camera very slightly off-center to the side opposite the way she is facing, which exaggerates her lean a bit. My studio camera stand had a rotating 360-degree camera mount, which encircled my lens and allowed me to rotate my camera freely in a complete circle. Camera tilting helps take your photo from static to dynamic, allowing your subject to seem like they are leaning more than they can comfortably lean on their own.

If you like, you can add a soft-focus attachment to your lens now, or maybe a white frosted or black vignette matte with a feathered oval opening cut in the center of it, via a matte box attached to the front of your lens. Adjust the position of your multiple portrait lighting to produce flattering, face-shaping, three-dimensional shadows on her face, with her nose shadow reaching about halfway to her upper lip, while being halfway between the edge and center of her upper lip. Set the flash power of your lights so as to produce a pleasing lighting ratio, 1:3 or 1:2, with one light brighter than the other.

The more of someone's face you put in shadow, the more of a slimming effect you can achieve. The viewer's eyes don't see what is in shadow, so the mind doesn't register it as being there, which is really helpful to know when photographing heavy people. Just put about a third of the face in shadow – your female subjects will love you for making them look thinner than they are! You can easily take a good ten to twenty pounds off of how people look using this tip.

Get your subject's attention, evoke a relaxed smile, and hit the shutter to capture a photo they will cherish for years to come. This is how Donald Jack and other Master Photographers taught me to take studio portraits. Tiny little steps, done one at a time, each one building on the others and improving the image as each is added, until perfection is achieved.

All of these adjustments only take a minute to do, once you get the hang of it. It is amazing how much of what you learn about taking good, pleasing portraits translates and carries over for use in wedding photography.

Be sure to do hand-posing on groups at weddings, too. Get rid of those meat cleaver views of the hands on the guys in your photos by having them turn their wrists just enough to show the front blade edge of their hand. The guy's hands seem to be extra noticeable, because they are usually surrounded by their black tuxes and this sharp contrast really spotlights their hands.

The skin showing on the back of each large hand on a guy is almost as big in size as the skin showing on their face in a group portrait at a wedding. The viewer's eyes and mind don't know where to focus, on the face or the hand, if the meat cleaver view of a hand is competing for their attention, too.

On posing groups, the tighter you can pack them together, the better. The bride and groom, which almost all group shots are built around, can be turned in slightly facing each other, while standing at floor level at the altar.

For small horizontally built groups, you also want to angle everyone else in on both sides of the newlyweds, so they are facing about 20 degrees in towards the center of the group. This slims them down in the photos and also helps you to pack them tighter together. It also allows you to hide one of each of the people's hands from view, which makes only half as many hands showing for you to have to pose.

I often told the guys in group pictures to move in really close, using my hands to demonstrate a squeezing together motion, and told them they should get rid of all the gaps between them, to the point where they feel they are really getting well-acquainted with the guy in front of them.

That statement always got a good laugh and caused everyone to loosen up and relax. This kind of interplay can really make it fun for people to get their photos taken. Relaxed people enjoying themselves makes for tremendous photos.

After everyone is packed tightly as a group, you can get them even closer by having everyone kind of lean in a little, from the waist up, towards the middle of the group.

Groups should be built vertically when they get big, not horizontally.

Building groups vertically is done by creating rows of people behind other rows of people, with each row a head higher than the row in front of it, which lets you clearly see everyone's face in the photo, as nobody's face is hidden by the person in front of them. Stagger the rows, so the heads are not directly lined up behind each other, obscuring the one in back. You build vertically by trying to build a pyramid, with the group getting smaller on each higher level of elevation.

For your front row, you might have three people on their sides, resting on their elbows in a horizontal position on the floor (these could conveniently be kids). A second row is built behind them of up to five people, who are moved in as close to the people in front of them as they can get. People in this second row are on one knee. This is really your base row, the three on the floor is a "freebie," filling normally unused space. They lean forward a bit from the waist up to close up the depth of the group from front to back.

Next, place another row behind them consisting of about four people, who could be seated on chairs or bending forwards at the waist and bending their knees slightly to lower themselves a bit to achieve the right head height spacing.

The final back row could be two or three people standing fully upright. Tall people are great for the back row, just be sure not to put really short people there.

Everyone in rows 2, 3, and 4 lean in slightly toward the camera to keep the group as shallow as possible from front to back, so you can achieve the best depth of field focus.

Focus on someone about a third of the way in from the front edge of the group, allowing what photographers call "depth-of-field," to render everyone in the group in focus, whether they are in the front row or the back row. It works well.

There are about fourteen people in this very tightly packed, well-arranged, vertically built group! If you posed this group horizontally instead of vertically, the head sizes of the individuals in the photo would only be about a third as big as the head sizes in the vertical group. Wow! What a difference! Photo 13-9 shows a wedding party of twenty people, quickly posed, tightly packed, and nicely grouped.

I've done wedding party groups using the four or five steps leading up to the altar to get the rows higher than the rows in front of them. I've done wedding party groups of over 24 people the same way!

When these same people were standing at the altar during the service, they had stretched shoulder to shoulder all the way across the front of the Catholic church where the wedding was held. They reached from wall to wall! By building my group vertically, I got them all in about a ten foot wide by six to eight foot deep area for the group photo, which illustrates my point about packing them in tightly.

On extended family groups, I was aware of any small children in the group who might be in the higher rows. If someone in their family doesn't hold them up so their heads are as high as the person holding them, they might not appear in the photo at all.

When doing extended family groups, I added one family at a time to the group, building on all levels simultaneously around the bride, groom, and their parents in the middle of the group. This keeps all the family groups intact within the extended family photos.

I used multiple lighting sources at weddings, too, the same way I would in the studio for portraits. The idea is to create the same three-dimensional lighting effects by casting those face-shaping three-dimensional shadows on my subjects' faces.

I used two computerized, top-of-the-line, pro-quality flash units, which were set so the flash on the camera was the master unit and the fill flash, mounted on a tripod pole, was the slave unit. That way, both flash units fired together when the shutter was tripped.

By dialing in the lighting ratio I wanted to achieve between my two lights, the flash units took care of achieving my desired ratio for me.

I have had some unsophisticated clients, who are not savvy about such things, and had them complain about there being shadows on their faces in their photos! Three couples complained about it in the course of only about a year in my small town of Richmond, Indiana.

I tried to educate those clients about why those shadows on their faces, that they were complaining about in their photos, were a very good thing. I told them those shadows made them look more three-dimensional in their photos and that it had a slimming effect, as opposed to flat, even lighting from a single flash unit fired from camera position. I'm still not sure they ever really believed what I told them about the multiple lighting sources being a flattering thing, though; all they knew was whether they liked the look or not.

I actually had couples who really hesitated to hire me because they noticed the shadows in my sample albums and weren't sure if they really liked that look or not. I figured, why fight it when it can cost me clients who might have otherwise hired me. Artsy-fartsy sometime isn't all it is cracked up to be, especially in a small town in the Midwest.

Finally, I just went back to flat, single-sourced defused and bounced lighting; with my on-camera flash mounted on a flip-flash bracket which kept the flash unit about eighteen inches directly above my camera lens, whether I was shooting the photo in horizontal or vertical orientation. It got rid of shadows cast on the walls behind my subjects by the flash. The bracket avoided any pink eye effects in my photos.

To get good smiles for my photos, I wasn't afraid to act a little goofy. I would often ask everyone in the group to say some off-the-wall, wacky word, instead of "cheese," to get those smiles. It really loosened everyone up and relaxed those uptight people. It got my relationship with them off to a great start. Trial and error told me which wacky words worked best to achieve what I wanted in the way of facial expressions.

People were always making comments about how I cut through the tension they felt when getting group photos taken. Some people dread being in group photos or even having their photos taken at all. If you can get rid of those feelings quickly, it will make you a hero to those involved in the group picture.

All this information usually costs people $500 to $1,000, in 1980's prices, to get someone with this knowledge to teach it to them. I bet it costs a lot more now.

It was almost as if the teaching Master Photographers at Winona just lifted the top of your head off and poured in tons of vital information, knowledge, and closely guarded trade secrets and techniques into your brain over those few short days the class was in session. It was taught in such a way, too, that you could return to your studio and immediately start putting the knowledge to work to earn your living with it.

I believe this next tip is easily worth the price of this book just by itself. That is saying a lot, but if you ever encounter a situation where you need it, having the knowledge of how to handle this particular situation can really save your day.

Some brides somehow have the innate ability to have their eyes closed in 95% of all the photographs you take of them. Sometimes, they already know this about themselves and will be nice enough to tell you about it in advance.

I've worked out a cure for this tendency. First, put your camera on continuous-exposure mode, so your camera takes photos at several frames per second for as long as you hold down the shutter button.

I had them totally close their eyes and keep them closed until I told them to open them. I started firing away and instantly told them to open their eyes. I held down the shutter button until their eyes were fully open. I repeated while shooting extremely close up, half-length distance, two-thirds length distance, full-length distance, and from about fifteen to twenty feet away.

Check the results to make sure you actually have at least one photo with her eyes wide open at each of those distances. If you don't, delete the images and shoot again. Repeat until you are successful.

These were my rescue master photos, the ones with the bride's eyes open. When I got an otherwise good photo, but the bride had her eyes closed in it, I rescued that photo by picking a rescue photo taken from the same distance.

Using Photoshop's clone tool, with both photos open, I cloned the eyes off the rescue photo over the closed eyes in the other photo. I selected my clone tool's source point on her eyes in the rescue photo, then cloned them over on the photo with her eyes closed. It only took a few seconds to do.

I've used this trick many times to save the day for the bride who is able to always get her eyes closed in the vast majority of her photos.

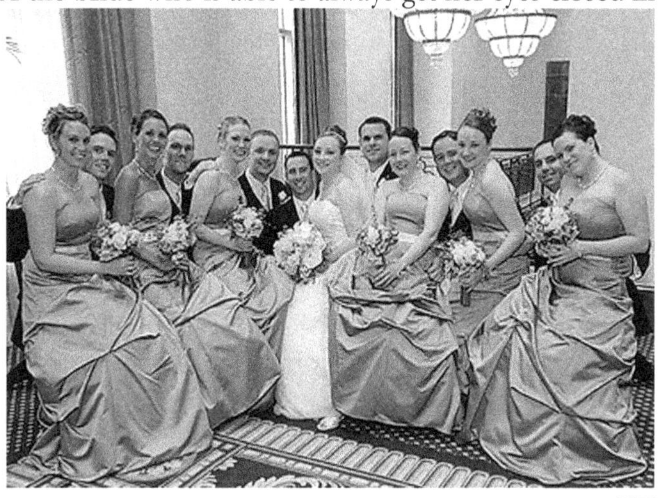

To change things up a bit on my wedding party group photos, I had all the guys go down right next to each other on their inside knee; half on one knee, the rest on the other knee. I had each of the girls in the wedding party sit on the "seat" created by the guy's raised knee and had her put her arm around his neck. Everyone else did the same. I now had a different looking, tightly posed group. I might have even started a romance. This pose, I did think up on my own.

Chapter 3: Advice for New Photographers

I've seen women spend an hour or more applying makeup, only to have their forehead and cheeks still be as shiny as a mirror when the camera flash fires. Their makeup was not doing the job it needed to do. If you keep an eye out for it, you can see the shiny spots on their face when the flash fires.

Photographers: be sure you carry shine-killing corn starch based powder foundation makeup with you to each assignment and don't be afraid to use it whenever you see a shiny face or head you need to photograph with flash. Those shiny skin surfaces might not be on just the girls, as some men's bald heads are shiny, too. Take the person aside and politely ask them if they mind if you apply some shine-killing makeup to the shiny area.

There were several occasions in my career when a piece of my equipment quit working while on assignment. I carried twice as much equipment as I needed, so if I couldn't solve the mechanical problem within a minute or two, I could run out to my car, fetch the replacement piece of equipment, and get back to work. I could worry about fixing the problem later, when time wasn't at such a premium. This strategy always worked out well for me.

I felt sorry for couples whose photographer showed up with only one camera and no backup equipment, because when his equipment quit working they were out of luck and missed out on having many wonderful memories captured. Always carrying plenty of backup equipment with me to each wedding I photographed was seen as the mark of a pro.

Most of doing a good job as wedding photographer is knowing what is going to happen before it happens, and when, and where, so you are always in the best position to capture each moment for the bride, from the best position. I always told my brides, "It's not nice to surprise your wedding photographer! If you have something unusual planned, you always need to make sure I know about it in advance, so I can be in position and can capture it from the best angle for you."

Unlike in other businesses, there are few repeat clients in wedding photography. Not having repeat clients is part of what makes wedding photography such a hard profession to get started in. I had to always be finding new clients, and I relied heavily on client referrals. It was extremely difficult and took me a while to get my reputation established enough to become fully booked all year round.

I had only one exception to the "no repeat clients" rule: a childhood friend of mine, who I'll call Fred L., who hired me to photograph all four of his weddings! Talk about a loyal customer. At his fourth and final wedding, I told him, "Hey, Fred, we have to quit meeting like this!"

One thing beginning photographers can do to become better is buy a second computer monitor and install it right next to your main monitor in a vertical position, on its side, so you can see your image both in a horizontal and vertical view simultaneously.

We grew up watching TV newscasters and other people on screens displayed as talking heads in horizontal formats all the time. My theory is that we've seen it for so long that it just seems natural and correct to us. I believe this bias affects how new photographers frame and crop the images they take. It is only natural that they would subconsciously frame and crop close-ups and half-lengths of individuals and couples as horizontals, just like they have seen on TV, movie screens and computer monitors all their lives.

It might even be gaining some acceptability today; since so many are now doing it, your peers of learning photographers probably won't notice it or point it out to you, but to experienced professional photographers, it make your work look amateurish.

When you can see an image side-by-side on both monitors, hopefully you will learn to automatically know when an image would look best framed and taken as a vertical. Vertical framing before shooting allows the photographer to zero in on the real money-shot, while leaving out the surplus background, which subtracts from the value of the photo and competes for your eye's attention. It's like when a new writer learns to edit out empty words like "that". Most sentences containing "that" read just fine without the "that" being present.

Trying to be helpful, I gave the following advice in a "Newbie Pro Photographer Facebook Group" about a horizontally framed half-length close-up of just a couple: "60% unnecessary and distracting background, and 40% money-shot. Your money-shot here is a tight, vertically taken close-up of just the main subject. :)" The unneeded background in this photo was a white over exposed sunlit sky. Being the brightest part of the image, it automatically pulled the viewer's eye and attention away from the main subject. Your eye is always drawn to the lightest part of a photo first.

Good, tightly cropped verticals are one of the marks of being a pro. Learn to crop in-camera before shooting, filling up the frame with your main subject. If you aren't comfortable getting up into someone's face to take such a tightly cropped photo, then zoom in to achieve the tight vertical in-camera crop from a comfortable distance. Pros learn to go vertical and tight automatically and zero in on their "money-shot" before they first take it.

The familiarity of the wedding day's routine as it unfolded was very soothing and relaxing. It was like dancing a dance I really enjoyed and knew how to do better in my own particular way than anyone else. I always challenged myself to see just how thorough coverage I could provide the couple, which turned the wedding into a game for me and made it more like play than work. It also prevented me from becoming burned out on doing weddings.

When things got rough, I always remembered: *the sun will rise again tomorrow, no matter what took place at my wedding today.* There was no need to put undue pressure on myself as the day unfolded. After surviving a few trials by fire, my hands finally quit shaking, and I gradually learned I possessed the capability to handle any rough spots as they arose.

The trick was getting comfortable in my own skin as a wedding photographer. With experience, I became unflappable during my assignments, which in turn, seemed to relax everyone else's nerves around me the entire day. They thanked me for making their day more enjoyable and recommended me to others because of it. Word of mouth and referrals are the best tools in a burgeoning wedding photographer's tool belt!

I never slighted the grandparents when taking photos at the wedding. Most grandparents don't get their photos taken very often by professionals, and lots of people have contacted me within two years after their wedding wanting more prints of the grandparents because one had just passed away. My photos of them taken at the wedding became cherished, and I became a hero for having taken those photos of their grandparent.

Outdoor weddings present difficult lighting situations. In bright sunshine, I used my flash unit to fill in the deep shadows on people's faces caused by direct sunlight. The flash compensation on my unit was usually set to minus two, which just filled in those shadows.

When I was mixing flash with sunlight, f-stop aperture settings controlled the amount of lighting my lens allowed in from my flash unit, while the shutter speed settings controlled the amount of natural light my lens allowed in from my surroundings. Remembering that rule made learning how to mix and balance those two light sources a lot simpler. To let in more natural light under a dark sky, I used a slower shutter speed. Using the right lighting combination made it hard for people to tell I had used flash.

Whenever possible, I always positioned people in open shade for their outdoor photos. When no open shade was available, I positioned them so they had the bright sun behind them to avoid them squinting or closing their eyes, and also to prevent there being harsh shadows on my subjects' faces.

Color Correction 101:

Have you ever had an image with a really strange color cast, but can't figure out how to tweak the colors to correct it? Let me introduce you to Adobe Photoshop's color ring-around tool. Use it to easily solve your strange color cast problems. In my outdated CS3 version of Photoshop, it is called "variations" and can be found under Image/Adjustment menus.

The color ring-around of the variations tool allows you to see your image in its current state in the middle of a circle of images, with other color variations of the image around it (More Red, More Green, More Blue, More Cyan, More Yellow, More Magenta), which shows what the image will look like if you add that color component to the cure.

Simply click on whichever image looks better. When you do, the image with the chosen correction now becomes the image in the middle of the color ring-around, and a new set of color correction options appear in the circle of images ringing the current image again. Repeat the process as many times as you want to, making new selections as often as you need, until you are happy with the results. All you have to do is choose the most natural-looking image among the choices each time.

A slider allows you to choose the strength of the color adjustment you want applied to the image in the middle of the ring-around each time you select the best-looking image from those available.

You always see a view of your original image, right alongside the image in the middle of the color ring-around, so you can compare your original image with how the image looks with the changes you have chosen. This makes it easy to tell if you are headed in the right direction or not. You choose to apply your ring-around corrections to the highlights, midtones or shadows of your image.

Color correction/white balancing = R:252 G:252 B:252 = white with detail not blown out.

If the true white in your image has no color cast, the rest of the colors in the image are accurate, too. Images with white wedding gowns can pretty easily be color-balanced for printing by putting the selection eye dropper in Photoshop on a portion of the white wedding gown that is properly exposed, with detail still visible. You then move your color correction sliders for red, green, and/or blue until all three numerical values are equal.

Bill Collins' 90 Day Get Better Quick Challenge for Photographers!

You will need two things for this challenge: a four-inch piece of gaffer's tape, and a lot of courage. Use the gaffer's tape to cover the screen on the back of your digital camera, so you can no longer see the screen after each shot. Guess what? The camera still works just fine! Next, set your exposure mode on your digital camera to completely manual, so you will have to learn how to control your camera's exposures by selecting your own exposure settings every time you take an image.

For the next ninety days, you are going to use your camera without the crutches you have used in the past: the digital screen and automatic camera settings to do your thinking for you. You're going to live with and learn from your results. These ninety days should very rapidly teach you to take great, straight-out-of-the-camera images which do not need rescuing or much tweaking in Lightroom or Photoshop. You will most likely become a real photographer instead of just being a post-production artist hobbling around using software crutches for years and years. I know it works, because this is how I learned back in the age of using film.

If you wish, you may exclude paying assignments from this exercise, substituting other sessions in their place. You can't hope to run on crutches and get very far, very fast; but take away those crutches and you will quickly learn to run at breakneck speed and amaze yourself. If you don't shoot every one of those ninety days, then just extend out the time until it equals at least ninety sessions.

My prediction is that by the end of those ninety days, if you've stuck with it and seen the exercise through, you will want to continue using manual camera settings for the rest of your life on nearly all your exposures, and you will be able to stop peeking at the back of your camera after every photo you take. You also might find you have been rewarded for your efforts by whacking two or three years off your learning curve towards becoming a knowledgeable professional photographer. Don't let the crutches built into your camera make you a dummy: take control and teach it who is boss.

Split receptions – where there is several hours of downtime between a ceremony and reception – were not a favorite with wedding photographers. The brides wanted to wait so they can party down at night!

One package I offered contained lots of printed photos for both sets of parents and the couple, but only eight hours of coverage. I finally had to change the conditions to eight **continuous** hours to discourage split-reception coverage from turning assignments into an unplanned all day gig. This policy prevented my clients from stopping the clock during the downtime between the two events, which I wouldn't be compensated for. I always stressed to my clients to buy the right package, because I never guaranteed extra time would be available if their allotted coverage time ran out.

If I could, I would sell my customers extended coverage at $100 per hour when their time ran out. I notified them half an hour before their coverage expired and encouraged them to get anything done they wanted recorded during that half hour, if they didn't want to buy extra time. That way, they didn't get caught off guard and could choose whether or not to purchase extra coverage.

At a super fancy hotel on Fountain Square in Cincinnati, the bride's father asked to purchase additional time, as he realized the amount of coverage they had purchased probably wouldn't be enough.

As much as I hated to do it, I had to turn him down, because I had another wedding booked for early the following day in Columbus, Ohio. I was already later than I expected at their wedding and I still had to get back home, recharge all my flash and camera batteries, and empty all my camera chips after burning the images to CDs, so they would be safely stored.

There just wasn't any way I could sell this bride's father extra time. I felt bad, but I really had no choice. I was committed elsewhere. They moved everything they wanted photographed to earlier in the evening and I ended up staying an extra half hour without charging them.

Nowadays, when I am out driving with someone and we pass a church, I can very often say, "I photographed four or five weddings there." Whenever I pass by a wedding venue where I've worked, I get a flash of memory of the assignment(s) I did there. I can't seem go anywhere in my entire tri-state coverage area without passing at least one church where I did a wedding. It kind of amazes me now when I think about it.

One thing I liked about marketing myself regionally was that I did not have to compete hard with other photographers for the same coverage areas; instead of hurting any one or two competitors' trade, I spread my business over three states.

As soon as a bride hired me, I emailed her my photographer's wedding questionnaire to fill out. The questionnaire contained all the information I needed to know to do a thorough job covering the wedding and not miss anyone important in the family group photos.

My questionnaire helped me predict how my day would unwind, and also helped me gauge what unusual events might transpire and how I could best prepare for them. It told me if any parents or grandparents were deceased, not attending, divorced, separated, remarried, or had new boyfriends or girlfriends. It told me if the divorced/separated people minded having photos taken together, and other helpful information about family politics that an outsider would not necessarily know.

The questionnaire did away with the necessity of a face-to-face pre-wedding final planning session with the bride, which saved another hour or two of my time per wedding and made hiring me more convenient for the brides, who were already stressed out enough as their wedding days approached. Life was getting simpler. During my final five to ten years or so, I met most of my bridal clients for the first time on their wedding day.

I used the completed questionnaire to diagram the bride's and groom's family trees. I noted any deceased parents so I wouldn't commit a faux pas by calling them up for photos, making the bride or groom sad. I learned that lesson the hard way! On the diagram, if the parents were divorced and didn't get along, I marked it by putting an "X" between them, meaning "keep them apart." For example, above the bride, I might list her parents like this: "mom X dad + girlfriend."

Above the parents I would list grandparents and whether they were couples, widowed, divorced or alone. To the right of the bride I would list her sisters and whether each had their own family, and to the left of the bride I would list her brothers and whether they had their own families. I did the same for the groom and his family members.

Using my wedding questionnaire info and knowing my master pose list by heart made it possible for me to move through the group photos in only twenty to thirty minutes. Everyone always appreciated how quickly I took the photos after the ceremony, because all the bridal parties wanted to get on to the reception as quickly as possible and not spend a long time taking photos.

This book's cover photo, of the groom dipping his bride in front of the lighted night water fountain, did not happen as it is depicted. The bride and groom part of the photo was taken roughly in this location, but during the daytime and with a "No Parking" sign accidentally appearing in the background, without any fountain.

Using computer software, I combined the night photo I later took of the nearby lighted water fountain, as the background for the bride and groom's daytime photograph. The most difficult part was making the bride's veil transparent enough to see the lighted fountain through. This is the one time I spent over two minutes Photoshoping an image. I saw the possibilities combining both images gave me. I like that photo enough, fourteen plus years later, to give it the place of honor of being my cover photo for this book.

This is a good example of one photographer stealing another photographer's pose when he saw it and liked it. I was with the wedding couple at the renovated Art Deco Union Terminal Train Station in downtown Cincinnati. I saw this other photographer create his groom-dips-bride pose right in front of us, while my wedding couple and I waited for our turn at the location in front of the train terminal.

When the other photographer and his couple moved on, I copied the pose I had just seen him create. I used the pose from then on, too. Photographers are some of the biggest copycats in the world, myself included!

Unlike a lot of professional photographers, I never felt the desire to submit photos to photo competitions. I never really considered myself very creative. My lack of a desire to enter competitions is the reason I never considered trying to become a Professional Photographers of America's Master

Photographer, as you have to be awarded several print merits for winning judged competitions against a nation full of other PPA member photographers to qualify.

Some studio photographers seem to spend months each year just thinking up, taking, and preparing their competition prints. It seems to become an art form in itself. This prospect never tripped my trigger.

Beating my own drum wasn't something I felt I needed to do, as my customers were always only too happy to beat it for me, by posting tons of online endorsements to various wedding-vendor-related websites. I felt word-of-mouth referrals and reviews were the best way to get assignments without having to spend a fortune on advertising or distinguishing yourself with a lot of fancy awards.

Often I even had the fleeting feelings I was somehow some kind of fake in what I did with a camera, even after all my top notch professional training. Let me tell you, feeling like that sure will keep your ego and feelings of self-importance at bay!

I'm a pretty quiet fellow, overall. If I don't have something to say, I keep quiet. On average, I probably don't say over 700 words per day, unless someone directly engages me in a conversation which especially interests me. I talked at weddings more than I normally did, usually while posing and directing groups for photos. Most weeks found me hoarse and on the verge of losing my voice about halfway through the group photos, and I had to struggle to make myself heard. I just muddled through as best I could.

Chapter 5: Handling Difficult Situations

Near the end of a nighttime reception at the Shriner's Club in Richmond, Indiana, one guest, who was seated at a table, suddenly knocked his neighbor onto the floor, by sliding sideways into him.

An all-out fistfight ensued, which lasted for several minutes. Many blows were thrown, with several guests wrestling on the dance floor. The DJ and groom finally jumped into the fray and managed to separate the combatants and settle things down.

A few minutes later, however, it all erupted into violence again! This time, several troublemakers – including at least one woman – were physically expelled from the building. Verbal threats flew back and forth from all involved. The bride was reduced to tears and everything came to a complete halt, while she retired to the restroom to regain her composure.

The mayhem shocked me. I had quickly debated whether I should be photographing the fist fights or not, as such situations had never been discussed in any of my training. Instinctively, I decided against taking those fight photos.

My coverage concluded shortly thereafter. When I exited, I saw at least a dozen deputy sheriffs, flashlights held high, checking the backseat of every vehicle in the parking lot. They were making sure nobody was waiting to waylay someone violently when they went to their cars.

The next day, the groom called me and apologized, explaining that the guy who started the fight was one of his relatives, who had a habit of starting trouble any time he got drunk. The groom wasn't at all surprised. He said they had had doubts about inviting him to the wedding, but had ultimately decided to invite him and hope for the best.

He asked me if I had managed to get any photos of the fistfights, because, if so, he would enjoy seeing them. I told him that I had instinctively decided against capturing it and that I made a habit of only photographing the good times. Again, it's never nice to surprise your photographer. If I had been brought into the loop regarding this guest or the potential for a fistfight, I would have known how to handle it.

During my first year of photographing weddings in Connersville, a bride actually came on to me at her own wedding! Everyone had just arrived in the church basement following the group photos after the wedding. The bride approached me and said she had another photo she wanted taken, showing a full-length rear view of her wedding gown all fanned out. So, we went back to the sanctuary and took the photo.

On the way back, she stopped me briefly in the deserted and dimly lit hallway, looked me in the eye, and smiled flirtatiously. She ran her fingers around my tie repeatedly, commenting on what a pretty tie I was wearing. She really shocked me by planting a more-than-friendly kiss on my lips.

We decided we had better rejoin everyone else. Nothing more ever became of it, but I did find it interesting and a bit tantalizing. I don't know what brought it on, but it definitely isn't something I ever forgot. I wonder if her hubby knew he'd better be keeping a really sharp eye on his new bride?

About a month later, while I was delivering my sales pitch to her, a bride-to-be asked me matter-of-factly if I'd be interested in taking my services out in trade. That was an easy decision: I thanked her for the offer, smiled sheepishly, politely declined her offer, and awkwardly changed subjects back to my sales pitch. Her offer had caught me totally off guard.

She must have been strapped for money, because she ended up not hiring me. Maybe she shopped around a bit more and found a photographer who was interested in her offer? I never had anything like that ever happen again, but I imagine other photographers have had similar experiences. I guess money isn't the only tradable commodity in the world.

Any special church rules governing where photographers could stand to take photographs need to be known before arriving at the church. At a Catholic wedding in Cincinnati, the priest stopped the service to ask me, from the pulpit, to move to the rear of the church. How embarrassing! I was two or three rows in front of the last row of seated guests.

Usually, Catholic churches are the last to limit where photographers can shoot from. Later, the bride apologized for failing to tell me about the church's rules about where I could stand. The priest had told her, but she had forgotten to relay the information to me.

Another church in Cincinnati had a strict rule that wedding photographers could only photograph from the last row of seats in the church, which was against the rear wall. That church really enforced the rule on all photographers, too. It was as if they had nuns stationed there to whack your knuckles if you disobeyed!

One of the largest churches in Indianapolis, located about halfway up North Meridian Street, had a small sanctuary in the basement where they held small weddings. They made me take the ceremony photos from twenty feet outside the sanctuary. As always, I used my long zoom lens, with no flash. My camera was mounted on my pro-quality tripod to steady it. I zoomed my lens in to where it was as if I was inside.

At a wedding at Oak Hill Mansion, in the Carmel section of Indianapolis, I found after the first few exposures of the pre-wedding group photos that the rechargeable batteries in my electronic flash units were weak. The batteries took ten seconds to fully recycle, and I knew there was no way I could do an entire wedding assignment with these batteries.

After photos, there was still about an hour left before the ceremony, so I took my leave and drove about a mile up the road to a drugstore. I quickly bought about $50 worth of non-rechargeable AA batteries for my flash units, which I used to complete the assignment. I replaced all my rechargeable flash batteries with new ones the next day.

Having my wedding film developed and proofed by a pro color lab always worked out fine in the age of using film, except for one catastrophic time. It was a Monday morning when the pro lab in a nearby town, which ran my wedding film, called to inform me they had accidentally run all my wedding film from the preceding Saturday's wedding through the chemicals twice. The negatives were so densely overdeveloped I could hardly see through them.

It was extremely difficult for the pro lab to get acceptable finished prints from these negatives, even with their high-powered enlarger. A negative of normal density would be exposed to the enlarger's light for just a few seconds. These ultra-dense negatives required an exposure of more than five minutes each to make a print. Since they had screwed up developing my film, I made them print the negatives, because their enlarger was more heavy duty than mine.

My customer received my apology for the color lab's mistake. I explained what had happened and how it had been beyond my control. I volunteered to give them anything they wanted or do anything they wanted me to do to try to make the situation better.

As a member of the Professional Photographers of America, I had the PPA's indemnification insurance against omissions and errors, which would even pay for totally restaging the wedding for new photos, including paying for the travel expenses for all the important people in the photos to bring them back for the restaged wedding.

Fortunately, my customers seemed to feel the finished photos produced by the photo lab were of acceptable quality, so we didn't have to go down the road of restaging and photographing the wedding again.

That was as close to total disaster as I ever came, while shooting film. It wasn't my fault in any way, and all I could do was try to make it right with my customer.

At my own first wedding, the main photographer, who was supposed to photograph the wedding himself, sent a flunky instead, who was somewhat soused upon his arrival.

He must have photographed the wedding with the aperture on his camera's lens wide open, by mistake, because all the images he took were terribly overexposed and decent prints couldn't be made from them. So, I've been on the receiving end of this exact same situation myself and know what it feels like. Maybe that bad experience is part of why I always did my absolute best not to screw up in any way on any wedding assignment.

My GPS proved to be totally a must-have device when doing weddings. I was always going into towns and areas of the big cities where I hadn't been before. I also had to be able to go directly from the church to the reception site without any delay at all and without getting lost. Time is really at a premium then, and I had zero spare time to hunt for my reception destination, usually in the dark.

For my wedding photo slideshow, I copied the images from my camera chips onto my computer with a software program I had purchased online, called Thumbs Plus, which automatically sorted my images by the time they were taken down to the second. No matter which of my two cameras I had used to take the photo, each photo appeared in the right order in the slideshow Thumbs Plus automatically created.

All the wedding images were downloaded onto my computer by the time the bride and groom were introduced at their reception. When they sat down to eat their meal, they got to enjoy seeing the laptop slideshow of all their wedding images I had just taken. Boy, talk about instant gratification!

It was nothing to see both sets of parents and all the girls and guys in the wedding party grouped around the computer, watching the slideshow between the meal and the time the festivities got underway. There were different people watching the slideshow all night. I always tried to capture their reactions to some of the funnier photos.

Back then, I think I was about the only wedding photographer in the Indiana/Ohio/Kentucky region to be doing such a computer-based slideshow at the reception. I never heard of anyone else doing it, at any rate. If the reception facility had a digital projector and screen available, I hooked in the computer and threw the images up on their big screen for all to enjoy as wall-sized images.

Later during the reception, as my camera chips filled up, I dumped them into the computer to update the slideshow with the most recent reception photos. Before I left, I handed the bride a CD I had just burned for her, which contained the entire slideshow for her to take on her honeymoon.

There is nothing like being able to enjoy your wedding and reception photos while on your honeymoon, right? The slideshow at the reception allowed me to showcase just how good a photographer I was to everyone present and was a memorable advertisement of my coverage. You just can't get better marketing!

It wasn't at all unusual for the father of the bride to shake my hand on my way out of the reception hall, at the end of the night, in order to press a folded $100 bill into my hand, as he sincerely thanked me for all I had done. When that happened, I knew I had truly succeeded in pleasing everyone there. Often, people huddled outside smoking when I left the reception, would call out to tell me what a wonderful job I had done that night. Great way to end an evening!

There was one time, however, when the slideshow at the reception nearly backfired on me. I uploaded and displayed the images without checking them individually. I was too occupied, taking new photos, to be able to check them all.

The only photos not displayed were those on the last couple of memory chips still in the cameras at the very end of the reception. Those images just got dumped into the computer at the last minute, then the entire slideshow was burned to a CD for the bride and groom. Those last images were never shown in the slideshow for everyone there to see.

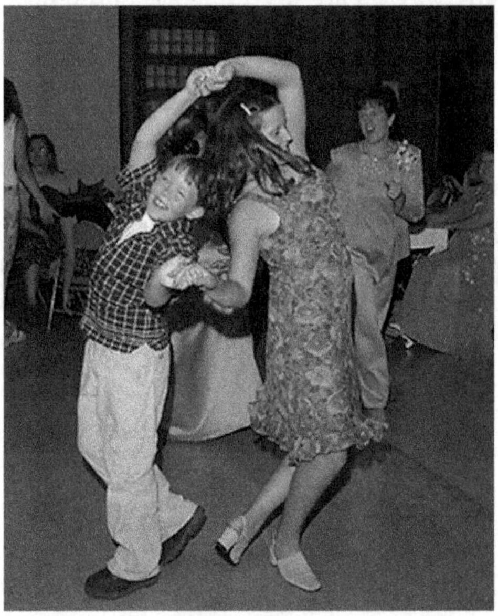

I often saw couples, usually a couple of female guests, or kids, do a hands-locked-together, high-over-their-heads, backwards spin while dancing at receptions. When I saw them doing these spins, I cued in on their spins with my camera, watching for their hands to go up in the air to tell me when to hit the shutter, in order to nail them in perfect position (facing away from each other, backs together, arms fully in the air with their hands locked together). Soon, I had gotten good enough that I never seemed to miss catching their spins at the perfect time.

One day, the groom from my previous week's wedding called me with deep concern in his voice. "We need to have our photo CDs replaced, because there's one image on these we can't allow our parents to see!" he exclaimed.

He went on to describe the image I described a few paragraphs ago, of the backward-facing spinning girls. It turns out that in this instance, one of the girls, who happened to be well-endowed, had been wearing a tube top, and during their spin, her tube top had totally slipped down, leaving nothing to the imagination for the briefest of seconds – seconds which I had happened to capture on film, without knowing it.

I hadn't even been aware of the flashing when it happened, as I had been keying in on their hands to know when to take the photo. I would venture that none of the other dancers around them at the time were even aware of what had happened.

The worried groom gave me the frame number of the offending image. I told him how sorry I was that it had happened and apologized for putting him in a tight spot. I explained how it had not been at all intentional on my part. I hadn't even noticed the "clothing malfunction" when the photo was taken, because I had only been watching their hands through my camera lens.

After I hung up the phone, I immediately deleted the offending image file from my computer, burned him five new CDs without the image, and fired them off to the newlyweds right away so they could get those CDs out to their parents.

Thankfully, this awful, potentially embarrassing accident happened near the end of the reception, so the image only got burned onto the CDs and had not been displayed live to people watching the slideshow at the reception. Whew! What a close call!

I always carried a fifteen feet long by five feet wide flat black cloth with me to weddings. Churches that had baptismals would often have a sheet of plexiglass across the front of it at the altar, which would be like a mirror when my flash hit it during group photos. When I encountered this situation, once or twice a year, I would cover the plexiglass with the black cloth using big squeeze-controlled black metal paper clips before doing group photos. It worked wonders and saved the day.

Once when I was using off-camera flash, the height of my flash was too low. The rear of the altar had some tall artificial shrubbery there on pedestals. After the wedding, it was pointed out that those shrubs had cast shadows on the walls near the ceiling behind the altar. I had to spend hours working in Photoshop to get rid of those shadows that were the shape of the leaves on the shrubs in all the photos of large groups.

I would transfer images from my camera's memory chip to my computer, in order to create a slideshow. Once, when I did this right after the ceremony, I received the error message, "Chip contains no files!" I tried it a couple more times, but got the same message each time. I ran the image file recovery software program I had put on my computer, and in about a minute all the images were safely rescued and copied over onto my computer's hard drive.

My images always had file names that were the time stamp of when the image was taken in an "hour.minute.second" format; for instance, a photo taken at 12:38 p.m. might be automatically named "12.38.46." The only damage from my image memory chip crash was that the rescued image files were all automatically renamed 0001.jpg, 0002.jpg, etc. by the software, instead of having the file names be their time stamps. Those "hour.minute.second" time stamp file names kept all the images in their proper order for the slideshow, regardless which camera they had been taken with. Thankfully, I could just rename those files manually after the wedding day to put them back into the proper order. Another bullet dodged!

I realize now that by being so well educated and experienced in my field, that I was able to confidently handle tough situations as soon as their arose; which kept me from having a lot more hair-raising stories to tell in this book.

Chapter 6: My Early Years

Buckle up your seatbelts. We are off on a wild ride down memory lane through my world as a professional wedding photographer for about 45 years. Very few people ever get to glimpse into what photographers see, do, and encounter in carrying out our wedding assignments. I'm inviting you to enjoy just such a glimpse into my world and to see it through my eyes.

Back to the Beginning:

My dad, Robert Emerson "Cy" Collins of Connersville, Indiana, was a creative part-time photographer while I was growing up. He was a tool and die re-builder and repairman for Stants Manufacturing Company, as well as an extremely good woodcarver.

When I was growing up, my bedroom windows were covered over with thick black tarpaper. It was pitch black inside when the light was off. Dad used my bedroom as his darkroom to develop and print the photos he took. Therefore, I grew up never afraid of being in the dark! I always just figured that if I couldn't see the boogeyman in this pitch darkness, then he couldn't see me either.

I was never nearly as creative as my dad. I became an accomplished photographer and was technically spot-on in all that I did, but not anywhere near as creative as Dad.

In Dad's day and age, during the 1940's and 50's, people didn't hire photographers to go to the church to photograph their weddings. At best, they would stop by our house following the ceremony and have a couple of photos taken of themselves in their wedding attire.

Dad had a tan-colored floor-to-ceiling curtain to serve as a backdrop. He would slide the curtain across a wire which hung just below the ceiling whenever he needed it to take photos. Hot floodlights in bowl-shaped metal reflectors were used as the light source for the photos.

Throughout our time growing up, my older brother, Tim, and I were both frequently dressed up in costumes by Dad and used as photographic models when he was feeling creative.

As a preteen I started taking a lot of photos, so Dad started buying me 100 foot long bulk rolls of 35mm black and white film that each contained about 1,000 exposures. I burned through one those bulk rolls of film every three months or so, just taking photos of other kids around the neighborhood. He taught me how to cut and load my own 35mm film canisters from the big roll of bulk film, how to mix my chemicals and develop my own film, as well as print contact sheets of everything I shot.

In high school, I always had my 35mm camera with me. When the teachers would post five or six blackboards full of notes we should copy and study, I would wait until the end of class and simply photograph each section of blackboard. Others had spent thirty minutes hurriedly scribbling all the notes down for further study. “Snap, snap, snap, snap” went my camera's shutter and I had my notes the easy way.

When I was growing up in the 1950's, "Leave it to Beaver" was a popular TV show my family enjoyed watching. I was fortunate to have a family life much like Beaver's. Life was so simple back then.

My first introduction to wedding photography was in 1964, when I was a year out of high school, by Osia Williams, owner/publisher of the Tennessee Pictorial Dispatch, a weekly regional newspaper I worked for in Cookeville, Tennessee.

Ms. Williams would make me go with her on Saturdays to churches where weddings were just ending and have me take group photos of the wedding party, bride and groom, and a few family photos.

She had worked out all the details of the photo-taking with the families in advance of our arrival. It seems that the added income she got from selling the families copies of the photos I took helped keep the Tennessee Pictorial Dispatch financially afloat.

We still used 4x5 Speed Graphic press cameras. They held metal or wooden film holders, which each held an unexposed sheet of black and white film on both of its two sides. Man, back then if you went to a wedding with five film holders – a total of ten shots – you were really loaded for bear!

One thing Osia taught me, which not even the Master Photographers seem to teach, was how to pose women's legs to look flattering in photos. I guess it takes a woman to understand and teach leg posing. It is not a big issue with long dresses, where the legs don't show, but on shorter dresses it makes a big difference.

Osia Williams taught me to pose women the way fashion models stand: rear foot turned outwards, with the heel of the other foot placed slightly in front of the instep of the rear foot, toes turned towards the camera. I stood the bride at a twenty to thirty degree angle – from facing head on, for slimming purposes.

This leg-and-foot-posing technique prevented the look you sometimes see in photos where a woman's legs looked like two beanpoles stuck straight in the ground with an unflattering open space between them. Instead, they looked graceful, with no gap showing between their legs. The legs were nicely sculpted to appear smaller, with very elegant and feminine lines.

When doing group photos at weddings, it took less than a minute to demonstrate this stance for the ladies, when short skirts are present, and have them assume the stance. I always made a point of telling them I was posing them like this so they would look their best in the photos.

A year later, I moved back to my hometown of Connersville, Indiana, where I photographed weddings while also working in various local factories. Wedding photographers were extremely few and far between back then. Maybe this was because, back in the 1960's, very few people were willing to accept responsibility for the photos (and possibly screwing them up, which was so easy to do back then!)

My professional training was acquired by attending a lot of wedding photography seminars and multi-day wedding and portrait workshops in the big cities throughout the Midwest, conducted by some of the country's top Master Photographers.

Once I even slept overnight in a parking lot in my van in Indianapolis, while taking a five-day portrait workshop taught by Donald Jack, world-renowned Master Photographer from the Omaha, Nebraska area. He taught me on three different occasions and I credit him with a lot of my training and style.

One lesson Donald always tried to teach never took with me. He would tell his students, "Your job as a photographer is to take as much of your customer's money as possible and move it from their pockets to yours!" This lesson always rubbed me the wrong way. I rebelled against it throughout my career, always offering as much value in my wedding photo packages as I could, while keeping my prices low enough I felt comfortable with them and brides never complained.

In Master Photographer's Workshops, we were taught, "Charge whatever the market will bear. If nobody is complaining about your prices being too high, then they are not high enough. Raise your prices gradually until people start to complain, then back them off just a notch. This is how you set your prices."

Donald Jack would always asked his students, "What are the most important and most often-forgotten photograph you can take at a wedding?" His answer was: photos of both the bride's and the groom's father, each with his siblings and with his parents, if they are present. Mr. Jack always claimed these photos were instant and constant revenue additions which should never be overlooked.

He said the bride's father was the most neglected person on the wedding day. He was just there to pay for everything. I was also taught that, sometime during the slow part of the reception, I should get Dad aside and have him totally empty his front pants pockets. I'd sit Dad in a chair, have him pull both empty front pockets inside out, and hold them there for my photo, showing just how broke poor Dad was by the end of the wedding! (One father had a roll of $100 bills about three inches thick in his pocket!)

These top PPA Master Photographers taught workshop groups of about ten students at a time in each big city during their three or four month cross-country teaching tour. We learned everything about how they went about practicing their craft.

The one thing all the Master Photographers taught is that wedding photography is about telling the story of the couple's wedding. Like all stories told, it needed a beginning, a middle and an end. . We were taught to end our coverage with a photo of the bride and groom outside waiving goodbye to their parents; even if it had to be staged way before they were ready to actually leave.

We were taught the more "circles of influence" you establish in the community around you, the more your business will thrive. This might have worked against me, as I am by nature not a joiner, and I never belonged to any lodges, clubs or civic organizations which might have helped me network.

Over the years, I took little bits of knowledge from all of my Master Photographer mentors and combined those individual parts into what became my own personal style and approach to practicing both the craft and the business end of photographing weddings.

In my later years, I would still attend training sessions every now and then, just to make sure I wasn't being left behind on any front, and to make sure my style was still up to date. It was always encouraging when I came away with the feeling I could possibly have taught the course myself.

When I was in my early forties, I studied at the Professional Photographers of America's Winona International School of Professional Photography, which was located in Chicago, Illinois. It has since been relocated to Atlanta, Georgia.

It seemed like it was always the dead of winter when I was in Chicago studying photography. I learned how to retouch my own color negatives, to get rid of people's blemishes by using liquid photo dyes applied to the negative with a brush only a few hairs thick, and tons of other handy skills.

At the beginning of my career, I was extremely nervous. I had trouble trying to keep my hands from shaking. There was always a tight knot in my stomach, and I felt like I was under a lot of pressure while photographing weddings back then.

Gradually, I suffered through my trials by fire, gained confidence in myself, and learned the sun always rose the next day, no matter what mistakes I made! Getting professional training at the hands of several of the best wedding photographers in the country really helped me build confidence in myself.

Early on in Connersville, Indiana, I booked and photographed four weddings on one spring Saturday. They were spaced out just right to allow me to make it to all four on time to photograph the ceremony and take a few group photos. Back then, the Catholics had their weddings during mid-morning. Then it was on to two afternoon weddings, followed by an early evening wedding.

Gradually I suffered through my trials by fire, gained confidence in myself, and learned the sun always rose the next day no matter what mistakes I made! Getting professional training at the hands of several of the best wedding photographers in the country really helped me build confidence in myself.

Back in those days, when the cake had been cut, the bride and groom had danced, the bride's dance with her father had taken place, and the garter and bouquet had been tossed, coverage was over. It usually did not exceed the first thirty to sixty minutes of the reception, sometimes much less. You never heard of a photographer staying longer to photograph any of the partying down.

When I finally offered unlimited wedding day coverage, I had to quit booking more than one wedding per day, as unlimited coverage would often amount to eighteen hours or more per wedding, including travel time. Coverage often started at a beauty shop in the mid-morning where the girls would be recorded getting their hair done and makeup applied and end when the reception concluded.

One of the most beautiful and original wedding cakes I ever saw is in the collection of photographs at the beginning of the book. Yes, it is an actual likeness of the bride and groom as the cake topper! They told me they had run across a website for a company somewhere in Asia which made the cake topper based on a photo they sent in. Neat!

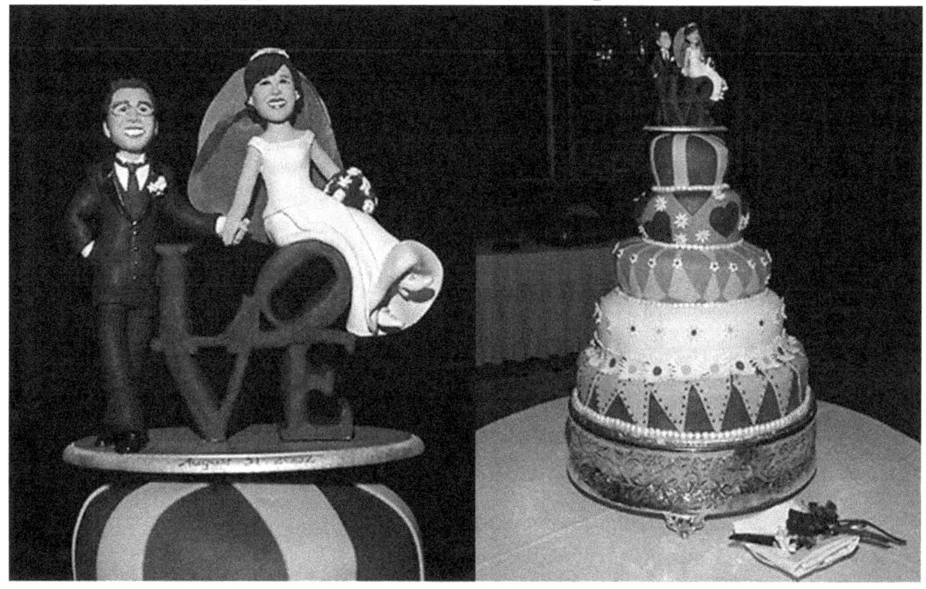

The importance of getting everything in writing and being paid up front was taught to me before I reached the age of twenty. I was just getting ready to take pre-wedding group shots at a small country church in Rushville, Indiana, when I saw another photographer coming down the aisle with his camera in hand.

He said the bride had contacted him and led him to believe he would be her photographer. It turned out I had already collected half of my money up front and he hadn't been paid anything. I ended up photographing the wedding while he left empty handed, stating he had learned his lesson about getting money in hand before going to a wedding.

Early on, I obtained half of my money up front and the remainder of the balance when the album order was placed. Later, I got smarter and made the entire balance due a full thirty days prior to the wedding. I made sure to get my cut before the client went broke overspending with other vendors.

My policies changed after I did a wedding for a young couple in Richmond who could not pay their balance when the time came to pay up. They had made a big deal in front of everyone at their wedding about being able to afford and hire a photographer, but then ended up not being able to afford my services! I finally wrote the balance off as uncollectible and learned my lesson.

A quarter of a century later, the same guy walks into my photography studio. He said it was their silver anniversary, and he wanted to get something special for his wife as a gift. He said I had done their wedding but they had never been able to get any of their photos back then.

I reached over to a stack of older 16x20 prints which had graced the walls of my studio at one time or another. I now kept them in a vertical flip-through display stack. I flipped through a few before coming upon a photo of his bride I knew was there.

He tried to bargain with me, but I held firm and told him the price was the full amount of the balance due on his wedding contract which he had never paid me. He said he still didn't have it and left empty-handed. Anyone else who had paid their balance could have purchased a 16x20 of their wedding for $100.

Early on, during my late teens and early twenties, I presented clients with a pose list of every possible wedding photo I could think of, and had them select 36 they wanted taken at their wedding.

Two teen sisters in Cedar Grove, Indiana – basically just a wide spot in the road south of Brookville, Indiana – decided they were going to have a double wedding at the local Catholic church. I did just about all the weddings there, through word of mouth and referrals.

Both sisters hired me to photograph their weddings, as two totally separate customers, and each gave me her own personal wedding pose list. So, talk about challenges! I had to take these two separate wedding pose lists and figure out in advance how to intertwine them into a workable workflow without missing any important moments for either of them!

This occasion was the only time I volunteered to attend the wedding rehearsal the night before the big day to see how everything might work out. It turned out each wedding party would be coming down opposite side aisles simultaneously.

I was more nervous than usual during this assignment, but everything came off without a hitch, and both brides were completely satisfied with the photos I took for them. Later on, I did the weddings of a couple more of their sisters (but only one wedding at a time!)

Within a few years, I developed a good photographer's "instinctive" eye. I could look at a wedding party of up to twenty people and know exactly when to hit the shutter to catch everyone paying attention, smiling, and with their eyes all open at the same time. This is no easy feat! At the time, I just took my ability for granted, but now I appreciate that I developed my talent. It got to where if something was wrong with posing, it just jumped out at me, so I could correct it. Minor tweaks made up front made huge improvements in the photos I took.

When I look back on one of my business practices from back then, I am amazed that I was successful at it! I used to offer a wedding album to my clients containing up to 24 8x10's. In addition, I added two complete matching wallet size sets of those photos at no additional cost for each of the mothers to have and enjoy.

What shocks me now, looking back, is that I would go to all those weddings with my camera – loaded with only a single 24 exposure roll of film – and take what I considered the 24 most important photos. I only took one exposure each!

The roll of film would be sent out and one 8x10 and two wallet-size photos of each exposure on the roll were ordered. This went on for a good ten years, with me delivering a perfect 24-photo album nearly every time. Nobody had their eyes closed or a sour expression on their face, and there were no bad exposures or missed photos.

This was successfully done over and over again, with me never even giving thought to how brazen I was being with such an approach. I just knew it efficiently kept my costs down, allowing me to keep my prices low.

Later in my career, I couldn't even begin to think about trying to do this. Over time and as I aged, my finely trained photographer's eye lost the ability to look at such large groups of people and know exactly when to hit the shutter to produce a perfect photograph each and every time. Later on, I had to resort to taking three or four shots of each group, just for insurance. Of course, everyone is more brazen in their youth!

As soon as I could afford it, I bought a Yashica-Mat 124-G double-lens reflex medium-format camera, which shot negatives about four times the size of a 35mm negative and had much better quality. You had to look down into the chimney on the top of the camera to see what you were photographing with double-lens reflex cameras like the Yashica-Mat.

Later in my career, I moved up and owned about $15,000 worth of used modular Hasselblad medium-format film cameras, which were considered to be the best cameras in the world. They were the overwhelmingly popular choice of camera for most professional photographers. Buying them used saved me about half of what I would have had to spend if I had bought them new. I spent a year hunting down and acquiring my cameras one piece at a time, a couple of camera film backs here, an eye-level viewfinder there.

Back in the pre-digital days, you actually had to know what you were doing with a camera in order to be successful as a wedding photographer, because you didn't get to see any of the results of your efforts until several days after the event was over, and there was little post-processing available to rescue a bad image. Cameras were totally manual then, too. You had to dial all the exposure settings in correctly by hand before taking the photos. Focus was manual, as well, with no auto-focus to do the job for you. I preset focus to ten feet for processionals, taking photos when the subject filled the viewfinder.

In film shooting days, using the medium-format Hasselblad cameras was quite expensive. Every time I hit the shutter, I had essentially spent a dollar (in 1985 dollars!) for the negative and a proof print, so I tried to limit coverage with film to from five to seven 24-exposure rolls of film, for a total of about 150 exposures.

I had my own color lab at my studio, complete with a professional enlarger, an automatic film processor, and a tabletop continuous feed color print processor capable of running up to 16"x20" size color prints which could process about eighty 8x10's per hour. I mixed all of my own chemicals for film processing and color print making and did all of my printing myself.

I've written an article that tells you what it was like to set up and work in your own in-house wet process color lab in the 19980's. If you'd like to read that article, email me. I wrote it because I realized that in a few years, everyone with a memory of such a thing would be gone. It was an experience I felt was worth preserving for future generations. I've also posted it on the internet in a few photography forums.

However, when I photographed weddings, I sent the film out to be developed and have preview prints made, because it was too labor-intensive to be worth doing myself. On my enlargements, I enjoyed being able to control the quality of my finished product from beginning to end. I don't know of any other wedding photographer in the region who did their own printmaking and negative retouching.

There was another part-time photographer who shot weddings in Connersville. He was quite rugged and handsome, and he seemed nice. Let's call him Mr. K. He knew how good my wedding photography skills had become, as I had shown him plenty of my work.

Years later, after I had established my studio in Richmond and had been practicing full time for a number of years, a lady who was with a bride who was about to hire me, said to me, "I am the reason this bride is here to hire you today. Do you know a photographer in Connersville named Mr. K? I was all ready to hire you as my wedding photographer several years ago, but I also went to see Mr. K. When he found out I was leaning towards hiring you, he told me I definitely didn't want to hire you. He said I'd be really sorry if I did, and I should hire him instead. He talked me into hiring him instead of you. My photos were so bad I still cry every time I look at them. I just wanted to make sure my friend here got a really good wedding photographer, which is why I brought her here today."

I was flabbergasted to learn about what Mr. K had done. It is amazing what you might find out years after the fact in a situation like this. It just goes to show you how cutthroat the wedding photography business can be, I guess. Last I heard, about ten years ago or so, Mr. K had started practicing wedding photography full-time and had established a photo studio back in Connersville.

When I was about nineteen, I was guilty of having raging male hormones kicked into high gear. At a wedding in southeastern Indiana, I was waiting in the entrance of the church for everyone to come downstairs from where they were getting dressed to line up for the processional.

This was in about 1965, and miniskirts were very popular at the time. I watched a couple of girls who weren't in the wedding party come down the stairs at the side of the entryway, getting an eyeful of bare leg as they came down the stairs, and I liked what I was seeing.

I must have been too obvious in checking them out, because suddenly a young girl piped up from behind one of them, "Hey, look, the photographer is looking up our dresses as we come down the stairs." Busted!

Immediately I hustled away from the stairs and went on down to the head of the aisle, hoping I could escape the embarrassment of getting caught red-handed. Lesson learned. Oh, those raging teenage male hormones can get you into trouble!

In the late '70s, I photographed the wedding of the bar manager for our local country club. Her husband worked with my wife at the Richmond State Hospital, so we would often talk briefly every time I went to the country club to cover a reception. I remember one time late in the evening, when she came over to me with a piece of paper in her hand. She said, "I'm not looking forwards to this." She showed me the piece of paper in her hand, saying it was the bar bill the bride's father was about to receive for having held an open bar for everyone present all night long. In today's dollars, it would have been for about $20,000! It is amazing how much liquor a huge room full of people can drink during the course of a night when they know it's all free.

I always thought of photographing weddings as like being an actor playing a part in a play; only the location and cast of characters changed from week to week; the story line always pretty well stayed the same. During your first 100 performances you usually sweated and worried about everything under the sun going wrong. After your 1,000th performance, you could play your part without worrying about almost anything, because you could play your part in your sleep.

I never assumed any airs of self-importance. For me, it was always just about getting the job done as unobtrusively as possible. A groom once told me the main reason he and his bride had hired me was my website reflected my wish to avoid the spotlight and do my job efficiently without intruding on the couple's special day.

I felt I really did not have any special talents behind a camera. I was no artist. I knew everyone else with my training could easily do all the same things I did. I always viewed myself as just thoroughly trained, with lots of experience; a really good technician at what I did.

I remember turning pro. I had been working for several years in a factory in my hometown of Connersville. That factory's owners had just announced that it was going to shut-down in with the next year or so. That was when my wife helped me decide to go full time with my studio I had sat up in a business building I had purchased in Richmond. It was open by appointment only, while I worked in the factory.

I didn't feel I was quite ready to make the leap yet, but she told me, "If you can't make it full time now, you probably never will be able to." I think it really shocked everyone in the factory that I was leaving, when I finally actually did it, because I had been talking about going full time with the studio for more than a couple of years. All the other factory workers just seemed to think, "Sure, keep dreaming!"

Going full time was a whole different ball game than just doing it part time. After the leap, there was a constant stream of bills to pay each month. I had to rely on my ability to promote myself and bring in enough paying customers each month to pay those bills. I started to worry a lot more, after it became my entire livelihood.

I had always had naive visions of having a balanced mix of income from doing engagement, anniversary and family portraits, weddings, baby photos, senior pictures, industrial and commercial assignments, copying old photos and renting tuxedos. I could see a steady stream from each of those coming in each and every week, in my mind.

After going full time with my studio, I found that I rarely did a baby photo. All my attempts to establish that market failed. The big box stores had that market cornered, with package prices that left no room for profit when tried on a smaller scale. Family photos were limited to maybe a couple a month. Anniversary sessions were even rarer. It all boiled down to senior pictures and weddings for the bulk of my income.

When opening the studio, I spend about $8,000 from my factory wages, to purchase a complete Scene Machine background projection system -- like the ones used to film the movie "Star Wars" -- that gave me hundreds of different backgrounds for in-studio sessions. That was many times more backgrounds than anyone else in town. It also meant that I could take winter scenes during the summer and summer scenes during the winter, without ever going outdoors.

I could even photography my subjects at any location in the world, too; all I needed to have in order to be able to do that, with the Scene Machine, was just a 35mm color slide of that location to project through my Scene Machine, onto the special floor-to-ceiling 12' wide Scene Machine screen mounted on the wall behind my subjects. I even purchased the special Scene Machine projection flooring that you could walk on without damaging it, for another $2,000, which allowed me to completely stand my subjects full-length, within the scene.

A special finely-meshed black screen was purchased and mounted directly over the projection background screen, in order to keep the studio strobes from washing out the projected image on the screen. Special light-modifying louvers were purchased and installed on the studio strobe units, too, to help do the same thing; together that was another $600 investment. My subject lighting for projected background sessions was done with a complete $1,400 Photogenic hard-wired pro-grade 4-light electronic flash studio lighting set. They were top of the line at the time and the only ones Winona recommended you buy.

I kept all my projected background slides displayed for client selection on five lighted slide-sorting light-table racks that each held fifty slides, all lighted at the same time for clients to select from. It took me a few months to learn to use the Scene Machine system to its full advantage.

At the opposite end of the camera room, I had a white floor-to-ceiling "infinity wall" built for seamless full-length high-key photos for about $1,000. I kept my camera mounted on a $1,000 pro studio camera stand, in the middle of the camera room, so all I had to do, to go from taking high-key portraits to doing projected backgrounds, was turn my camera stand and camera in the opposite direction.

I had invested, by my quick count, about $15,000 into my camera room, excluding the costs of my cameras. I wanted to be sure to be using as good equipment as any other pro in town. I had thought those investments would insure my success, but the top Master Photographers in town had a pretty tight grip on the senior picture and family portrait markets.

I always purchased high school senior mailing lists each year from professional list brokers. I received address mailing labels for all 1500 seniors in the ten or so high schools within a thirty mile radius. I mailed my full color advertising fliers to all the seniors religiously every year, at great expense, but that just didn't capture a big enough market share for me.

I could never get over about forty seniors to photograph each year, no matter how much I advertised. Everyone that I did senior pictures for seemed to love the variety I was able to achieve in their photos and being able to select all their own backgrounds, but my market share never grew. So, I ended up surviving locally by being able to capture way more than my fair share of the area's wedding market.

Chapter 7: Going Digital, Going Regional

In the last fifteen years of my career, professional grade digital cameras became good enough to do weddings. I was a full-time studio owner in Richmond, Indiana, doing all kinds of studio photography back then. The year was about 1998.

I was one of the very first wedding photographers in the Midwest to start using exclusively digital cameras at weddings. After successfully becoming a weddings-only photographer, I dropped all my other lines of photography and rarely even used the studio building I owned in Richmond. All my work was done on location in the big cities, at churches, and at reception sites in those areas.

I purchased my first pro model digital camera online. It was a used camera and came with a ten-day return guarantee, which I ended up choosing to use right at the end of the ten day span. I finally had come to the conclusion that this particular camera was just too early of a model and was not capable of producing the quality I needed, as much as I wanted to be able to use it to photograph weddings.

When I called the seller on about the ninth day of the return guarantee period, he was floored, because he had already spent the $2,500 I had sent him for the camera. He worked in a studio as an understudy to the main photographer. His boss ended up refunding my money, and I guess he probably then made his understudy repay him.

All my expensive Hasselblad medium-format film camera equipment was sold to recoup my initial costs for two pro model Nikon D1 digital camera bodies and three high-quality zoom lenses. As soon as they became available, I purchased pairs of new D1x, then D2 35mm single-lens reflex digital camera bodies every couple of years, as the quality and features improved. I sold the older equipment on eBay each time I upgraded, to help pay for the newer, more capable models.

At that time, the D1 bodies cost $5,000 each. I also had $2,000 worth of Nikon's best professional computerized flash units. I owned five flash units at $400 each and used one on each camera. Instead of changing batteries when they got low on power, I could just swap in a different flash unit with fresh rechargeable batteries already inside and be ready to go again. It took less than five seconds to switch in a new flash unit. This was important, because I never knew when my flash batteries were going to die or what important event would be happening when they died.

I eventually owned three of Nikon's best zoom lenses, which cost from $1,500 to $1,800 each, in 2001 prices. The fast low-light-capable telephoto zoom lens was mounted on one body and was used on a tripod. I only used it to take the ceremony photos without flash from the rear of the church.

The normal focal-length zoom lens was usually mounted on the second body, and I used it for most flash photography and small group photos. I used the wide angle zoom lens for doing large wedding parties and huge family group photos.

I purchased a professional $3,500 dye-sublimation printer. It was just like the printers used in kiosks at Wal-Mart and other chain stores where customers can print their own pro quality photos.

Each 8x10 print from the printer cost slightly over a dollar for materials used. My favorite benefit from using the printer was that I could receive a list of photos for a bride's album in the mail in the morning, tweak and retouch all the selected photos on the computer using Adobe's Lightroom and Photoshop computer software, and make the prints in just a couple of hours. I inserted those prints in the album and had the finished album off in the mail on their way to the bride by the close of the same workday. Now that's quick service! Being a weddings-only photographer, who only worked one day most weeks actually covering weddings, made this a possibility.

Proweddingphotos.com was created as my website, and I spent a lot of time and effort over the first three years online writing copy to convince brides to pick up their phones in Indianapolis, Cincinnati, and Dayton, Ohio and hire me.

By year three, the website was so successful brides were constantly hiring me without ever having met with me. If we did meet before the wedding, I made them come to me. I figured the more they felt they knew about me and my approach to wedding photography, the more likely they would be to hire me. So, I put as much information as I could about how I did business on my website.

Before long, proweddingphotos.com reached the topmost or second position on all the major internet search engines for each and every search term brides used to look for wedding photographers in Indianapolis, Cincinnati, and Dayton, Ohio.

I gathered a lot of useful information about what was happening on my website with the purchase of top-notch website traffic analysis software, which kept track of all visitors to my website, including what path each visitor took through the website and how long she stayed on each page she visited. The software showed me exactly what search terms each visitor had used to find my website and which search engine they had used. It even showed me where they were from, on what weekday and hour they had visited, as well as how many different times they had returned to my site. Having hard statistics like this sure beat just throwing up a website and hoping it was doing the job.

It wasn't easy to get my website to the top of the heap. It took months of trial and error, constant tweaking, and a lot of tedious hours spent learning about search engine optimization (SEO).

SEO is basically the science of fooling the search engine's computer into putting your site at the top of the heap of search results. SEO is really important, because if you are not in the top three search results when brides search, your website is unlikely to even be seen by 90% of internet searchers.

The one page which needs the most optimization is your website's home, or index, page. This is where everyone lands when they first enter your website. Getting to the top listing is achieved by trial and error and through a lot of fine-tuning over an extended period of time.

You have to figure out what percentage of your optimized search terms the search engine is desiring to see on your page. If those phrases or the words in them appear too many times, you are severely penalized by the search engines' algorithms for spamming the search engine. If those phrases don't appear often enough, your page will be ranked way down in the search results, where your site will rarely be viewed. Your website simply doesn't seem to exist to those seeking your services. Get search phrase frequency right, and it pops your page right to the top, so everybody finds you and checks out your website first!

I worked several hours a day for many months to reach the top of the search results for my regional market areas. During the first year my website was up, I spent as much time fine-tuning my website and adding content as I did photographing weddings and printing wedding photos. I also had to get lots of related websites to exchange links with my site, as the quantity and quality of links help the search engine decide whether your page is top dog.

Once clients started to find my website, I had to have content on my website that grabbed their attention enough to make them want to stick around. This had to happen within ten to fifteen seconds after they first arrived; otherwise, they were off to look at someone else's website.

My homepage had to immediately grab my visitors' attention and draw them deeper into my website. It's a simple concept, but I'm not saying it was easy! My website had to load really fast into their browsers, too, as they wouldn't stick around for half a minute as it loaded. People aren't patient.

While I was just a local photographer in the Richmond, Indiana market, I usually booked about 24 local weddings a year. At the prices I could charge in that market, that wasn't enough business to make full-time wedding photography a financial possibility there.

My goal was to become a weddings-only photographer, but to accomplish that goal I needed to expand to a regional market, which allowed me to increase my prices and still be charging only half of what photographers in that regional market usually charged.

When I first expanded from being a local to a regional wedding photographer, I felt I had to volunteer to go to the bride's home to make my sales pitch and show my sample albums. This usually involved me driving sixty miles or more each way, without being reimbursed for mileage, just to get a chance at being hired.

What I mostly encountered were brides who were just curious or shopping around between several photographers. A few other wedding photographers, who wanted to "shop the competition" to see what I was up to, had me visit them at their homes in Indianapolis. They always tried to play the part of an engaged couple to study my sales pitch and what I had to offer, but I could usually tell they weren't genuine potential clients within a few minutes.

Sometimes they even tripped themselves up, like one time when the supposed bride remarked, "That's exactly how you do it, too. Isn't it, honey?" And the cat was out of the bag!

Frequently, I found myself in a situation where nobody was even home after I had driven over an hour one way to meet with them. Sometimes we met at restaurants and I would pitch to them over meals.

People were taking such advantage of me that my wife finally put her foot down, saying that my constant traveling to do sales pitches was destroying our family life and it had to end. I was on the road to the big cities around me most weekday evenings trying to get hired, and it simply wasn't working. I wasn't booking enough weddings to make my operation profitable, especially with all the travel time and gas figured in.

When I was first getting started in Richmond, Indiana, I would pay to display my wares at bridal fairs, in the hopes of having brides line up to hire me. It never happened. It seems most brides who attend bridal fairs and bridal shows are just window-shoppers. I hated doing bridal fairs, and I never went that route in either Indianapolis or Cincinnati.

I put my entire sales pitch, which emphasized the benefits of having me photograph their wedding, how I viewed my job description, tons of sample photos, and a complete wedding which could be viewed as a slideshow, up on proweddingphotos.com for all the brides in the region to see.

Going regional was the best way to put my studio back in the green, and I decided to go for it, using the Bridal Guides in the big city markets to help me reach the larger amount of brides with my offerings, who lived in the big cities.

I took out the least-expensive advertising available in Indianapolis Bridal Guide, a black-and-white half-page advertisement. The Indianapolis Bridal Guide was published biannually, in February and September. In order to catch the spring engagement announcements for the rest of the year, I always chose to advertise in the February issue. The bridal guide ad cost something like $1,750 early on, but just a few years later the price had risen to $1,900 per issue, meaning I had to photograph two weddings each year just to afford it.

The Bridal Guides were given out to brides free of charge at all the wedding vendor locations throughout the entire greater Indianapolis area. All I tried to accomplish with the ad was simply to drive brides to check out my website.

I always thought of the Bridal Guide ad as a "monkey fist," which let me get potential clients to my website and sell them on hiring me there. Definition: a monkey fist is a big knot at the end of a thin rope used to get really thick ropes onto ships to anchor them dockside. The thin, lightweight, monkey-fisted rope can easily be thrown onboard from the dock, then used to pull the really thick and heavy ropes aboard to tie off the ship.

A major benefit of advertising in the Bridal Guide was it gave me instantaneous and continuous access to the Guide's web-based database of all the engaged brides who had signed up with the Guide to receive information from the Guide's vendors. Their database listed when and where they were getting married, and also contained their contact information and whether or not they were still shopping for a photographer. Everything I needed to know to make hay!

I only had access to this data as long as my ad was active in the Bridal Guide. There might be thirty to fifty leads for each wedding date who still needed photographers, with new leads being posted on about a weekly basis. All I needed was to get one of those bride's business for each wedding date, to be financially successful.

If the wedding date of a database lead was open on my schedule, I mailed my printed flier and a CD slideshow, complete with music, of a wedding I had done in one of the ritzy Indy locations, with group photos taken at the Soldiers and Sailors Monument, on Monument Circle, in downtown Indy, and other scenic locations. I would follow up with a phone call a couple of days later if they hadn't called me first.

The CD slideshow contained every single photo I had taken during the wedding prep, the wedding, gand the festivities at the reception. All the duplicate exposures I had taken for insurance purposes of the groups were removed, but other than that it was my complete record of one ritzy Indy wedding.

By seeing every single photo in the completed assignment, future brides could get an accurate picture of what they could expect when they hired me as their photographer. I pointed out in my sales pitch that inexperienced startup photographers often showed a sample album containing a mix of the best three or four images from a number of different weddings. Such a mix made it impossible for the customer to get any real idea of how consistent and thorough their coverage would be, whereas my materials were much more comprehensive and informative.

Each year, I alternated back and forth between advertising in the Indianapolis Bridal Guide and the Bridal Guide in Cincinnati, Ohio, to develop both markets simultaneously.

When my wedding schedule finally started filling up all the way and I was fully booked for the entire year, I dropped the bridal guide ads entirely and never saw any dips in how many weddings I booked each year. My website carried the day for better than ten years.

Looking back now, I believe I may have given the bridal guides too much credit for my marketing success. If a bride called from Indianapolis, I simply assumed she had found out about me through the ad in the Indianapolis Bridal Guide. A couple of years later, I started asking each bride -- when I talked to them on the phone for the first time -- how they had discovered me. To my surprise, most didn't mention the Bridal Guides. They mentioned having found Proweddingphotos.com.

Once Proweddingphotos.com rocketed to the top of the regional search engine results, I didn't seem to need the wedding guide ads anymore to stay busy. Also, referrals from my many satisfied big city clients and their families and friends contributed to my staying fully booked. I had finally arrived on the regional big city stage! I was totally amazed at having succeeded in what I had set out to do.

The biggest difference I saw in my business after successfully going regional was in the ease of getting hired. When I was working exclusively in the local Richmond market, I had to spend at least an hour with each and every bride just to get my chance to get her to hire me. Regionally, I might have to have a face-to-face pre-hire meeting with one or two brides per year at the most.

When we did meet prior to the wedding, I always made the brides travel to me. I quickly realized most of the brides would simply choose to give me their credit card information over the phone and hire me without the meeting, as soon as they found out they were the ones who were going to have to travel for the meeting.

What a difference between the competitive local Richmond market and working the greater Indianapolis and Cincinnati markets! In the Richmond market, back when coverage ended ninety minutes into the reception, it seemed like you spent almost as much time just getting hired as you did doing the assignment. Getting hired was more important then, too, because there weren't thirty to fifty brides fighting over my time like there was in the regional marketplace. If I didn't get that one and only local bride to hire me for her wedding date, I might not have had a wedding to photograph that weekend! But in the regional Indianapolis and Cincinnati markets, I was booked every single weekend months in advance.

Looking over 5,000 emails to potential clients, a particular email really grabbed my attention. The email heading was: "Top Ten Reasons Why You'll Want ProWeddingPhotos as Your Wedding Photographer!" It was responded to by many hundreds of brides. It replaced my flier mailings.

Anytime I got a bridal lead, I sent the bride this email, then followed up with a phone call a short while later. The email described everything which set me apart from all the other photographers they might hire. It basically contains the information I always told brides when I pitched to them face-to-face.

My offerings were structured so I made the $1,000 profit per wedding I wanted, with the idea of photographing one wedding per week to earn my living. Many big city wedding photographers seemed to earn their living by doing only about twenty weddings per year at twice or three times what I charged. Remember, photographers at that time were being taught to charge what the market will bear.

I felt I had to offer the brides a better deal to give them reason enough to hire me from sometimes more than sixty miles away, instead of hiring a local big city photographer. My pricing was less than half what the big city wedding photographers were charging, which considerably helped my image with potential bridal clients. I advertised myself as offering "America's best-value wedding photo packages!" and used the tagline, "Get three times the coverage for half the price big city wedding photographers charge!"

With digital coverage, I no longer had the cost of a dollar per exposure for film and paper proof every time I clicked the shutter. When I was providing digital coverage instead of film, about my only material cost was the roughly $100 I had to spend per wedding for the 36 8x10 prints and the album. Using digital cameras was liberating, too, as I no longer needed to limit how many photos I took for the bride.

I soon found myself taking up to 1,400 exposures per wedding, about a tenfold increase over what I could afford to do when I was using film. Now I could take thirty or forty photos of both the bride and groom's first dance and the bride's dance with her father. Wedding toasts? I could bang away with abandon, capturing the minutiae of all the interactions between those involved.

Because of the savings of not having the expenditures of film and paper proofs, I feel I basically got my digital cameras for free; they paid themselves off so thoroughly in the benefits over using film. The year before I went digital, I had spent $7,500 on film and $3,500 on paper proofs. My digital cameras cost me less than those expenses, and the digital memory chips were erased and as good as new for the following week's wedding.

By averaging a wedding per week, I was able to work one day per week photographing weddings, spending half a day later printing their finished album of photos. That way I could make my living doing weddings and not have to do any other kind of photography, an idea I liked quite a bit.

It was quite a jump going from the 24 weddings I was doing per year in Richmond, Indiana, with packages in the $550 to $600 range, to working with big city brides from both the Indianapolis and Cincinnati regions with higher-priced packages. Soon after going regional, I lost almost all my market share in the Richmond area, because the big city brides claimed all my wedding dates up to a year in advance, way before Richmond brides had even announced their engagements. Of course, there weren't many weddings per year in Richmond to lose, anyway: it is a small town.

One big city photographer I read about online, who was working in the same area as I was, charged $6,000 during the 1990's just to show up! His photos were then offered for sale in an a la carte fashion. I always felt he was simply marketing snob appeal to the wealthy, who hired him so they could brag about how much they had spent for him to appear.

My most popular package was unlimited wedding day coverage, with 36 8x10's of their favorite photos in an album to keep, along with five copyright released CDs containing every single digital photo I had taken. Over 95% of my clients chose this unlimited coverage package. It was priced in 2002 or so at $1,195 and in later years at $1,495.

Chapter 8: Unique Weddings

Have you ever attended a wedding in a cemetery? I have, twice. The first was at Spring Hill Cemetery in Cincinnati, Ohio, at an old, small limestone chapel on the grounds that was rented out for weddings. It is very nice inside and well-suited for a small wedding. You would never know you were in a cemetery after entering the chapel.

The wedding at Spring Hill Cemetery involved a young and exceptionally beautiful blonde Russian bride, whom the groom had brought over from Russia to marry. Her mother was able to attend the wedding, too. The bride spoke some English, but her mother didn't speak any English.

The second wedding I photographed in a graveyard was a reception at Forest Hill Cemetery's newly built (at the time) Family Life Center on the east side of Indianapolis. It was huge and elegantly magnificent inside. It had ornate inlaid marble floors and a stunning cut-glass chandelier almost twenty feet tall hanging in a bell tower three stories tall. The bell tower had huge windows spanning all three stories, so the lighted chandelier could be seen from the highway when you passed by at night. It was stunning! ==>>

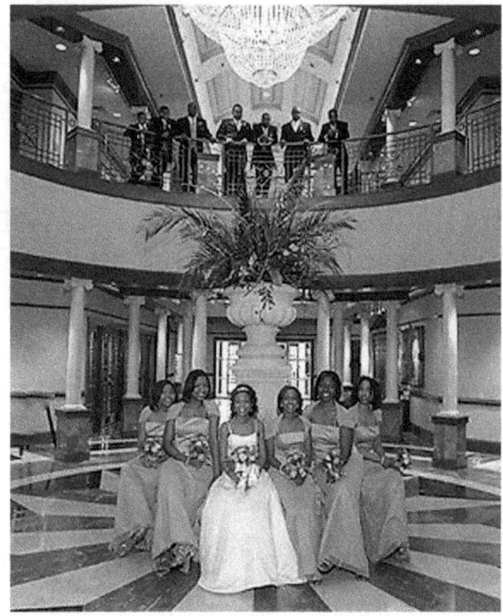

Twice, I've done Eastern Orthodox weddings. These weddings start with the priest leading the wedding party down to the altar from the rear of the church. The ceremony involves a lot of incense censers being swung back and forth by the chanting priest. The couples are crowned three times with something that looked like halos with ribbon streamers hanging from the back. Near the end of the ceremony, the priest lead the couple in circles around the altar several times. It was an interesting phenomenon to see and photograph.

A lot of Jewish weddings seemed to populate my wedding schedule in both Indianapolis and Cincinnati. Through photographing these weddings, I learned the bride and groom marry each other in a private ceremony before their synagogue wedding. The private ceremony involves just the bride, the groom, the rabbi, and the bride and groom's parents, who witness the couple signing their wedding contract. Some of the marriage contracts I've seen were hand-lettered and very fancy. They must have cost many hundreds of dollars to have custom-made.

The Jewish couples are officially married once they have signed the contract. They then went out and had a big wedding ceremony in front of all their family, friends, and guests. I always took plenty of good photos of the contract signing without using a flash, as these photos were considered an absolute must by Jewish couples.

At one Jewish wedding in Cincinnati, the bride's father kept coming up to me at the reception and taking me outside, where he had rounded up family members for groups he wanted photographed. He would keep me busy shooting various groups for a good twenty minutes at a time. We'd go back inside, then, about half an hour later, he would take me back outside for another twenty minute group photo session photographing entirely different groups he had rounded up.

This went on repeatedly for at least three hours. I don't think I have ever taken so many different family groups. There were probably fifteen groups present from various European countries, and it seemed like only a few people in those groups could understand English. I had to use hand gestures while posing them.

I have such fond memories of photographing Hindu weddings in both Columbus, Ohio, and Louisville, Kentucky. Some Hindu weddings have pre-wedding celebrations, lasting for up to a week, leading up to the wedding itself.

I never got to photograph any of the festivities prior to the wedding date, as the couples hiring me didn't want to pay for the extra coverage. I offered to cover those festivities, but only at my full wedding price of $1,500 for each extra day of coverage. At the weddings, I heard about how lavish those festivities had been by talking with the videographers.

Hindu weddings are very elaborate. The bride's family, as a group, met the groom as he arrived at the wedding site. The women blew repeatedly on seashells, which have been made into musical instruments, as a greeting to the groom, then lead him inside when the wedding started. The bride and her bridesmaids had already entered and had taken up their positions inside.

Once the groom was led inside, the bride, with her face hidden from sight (See Photo 8-16), circled the groom with her bridesmaids seven times. Both the bride and groom went to great lengths not to make eye contact with each other during this circling of the groom. When the bride finally stopped in front of her betrothed, after circling him seven times, they finally made eye contact. This eye contact is what signified their intention and desire to wed each other. I guess you could say that she was given seven chances to bail on him.

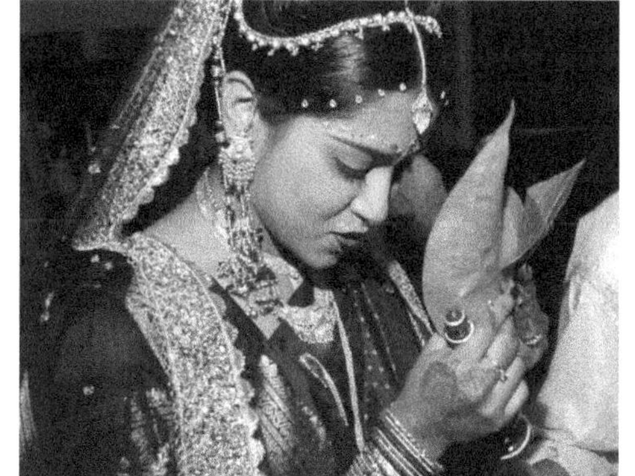

Everyone in the wedding party, including the bride's and groom's immediate families, then went to a raised platform with a Hindu priest, where they sat cross legged in a circle on the floor and took part in the wedding ceremony that lasted about two or three hours.

Everything they did was repeated either three or seven times. There was a lot done with rice, flowers, salt, and fire. The bride's and groom's arms were wrapped together with the groom's scarf by the priest, to bind them ceremonially to each other. At various times, they all got up and marched around the stage in a circle seven times.

During the entire wedding, the groom carried a coconut in a pouch on his waist, which symbolized fertility. I captured each stage as it happened and was repeated. At the end of the ceremony, I found I had taken about 500 photos of the ceremony itself, entirely exhausting a camera battery in the process.

After the wedding ceremony, the bride was taken to the hotel where the groom's family was staying. She was welcomed into the groom's family by what they called a salt ceremony, which involved coins and salt in a wooden bowl.

The bride repeated this ceremony with each and every member of the groom's family. The salt and coins were blessed again for each family member's ceremony. Each of the groom's relatives dug a coin out of the salt and handed it to the bride. I was told this was to signify that she was now considered by the person as her relative, and the coins represent the sentiment that money will never be allowed to come between them.

Of course, the cuisine at Hindu weddings was Indian. At her reception in Columbus, Ohio, the bride left the banquet hall at least once each and every hour to put on yet another beautiful, expensive Indian gown. The gown changes went on all night long and had to involve thousands and thousands of dollars worth of gowns. She wore a lot of gold jewelry and had henna designs imprinted upon her hands.

The groom had one of his shoes stolen by a small group of women during the reception. They snatched his shoe right off his foot and threw it out into the crowd, where it was tossed keep-away style around the room several times as the groom tried to get it back. Finally, a couple of young women approached him with the shoe, and they negotiated for about ten to fifteen minutes as the groom attempted to buy back his shoe for cash. The young women were expert hagglers, and they took great pride in getting top dollar from him for the return of his shoe.

I asked someone later exactly what had happened with the shoe being stolen. They said it was tradition, much like our garter toss. The more money the women could get out of the groom, the happier he would supposedly be with his bride. It was all done in good spirits and enjoyed by everyone present as they rooted for the women to keep holding out for even more money. I guess, according to tradition, he had to buy his shoe back in order to keep his bride.

I was rarely sick, maybe twice per decade, and I never missed a wedding because of illness. I did photograph a couple when I was feeling so badly I had to more or less go on autopilot. When I got the previews back, I could never see any difference between the photos I took on days I felt well and the weddings I took on autopilot.

On at least twenty weddings I did, the officiating minister marrying the couple was the father or grandfather of either the bride or groom. This happens a lot more often than most people realize, but every couple I have seen married by a relative seem to think it is special and unique to them.

In about 2002, a couple of gay men hired me to photograph their commitment ceremony at a large church in Indianapolis. It wasn't legal for them to get married, but they decided to have a big public ceremony and celebration of their commitment to each other. It was a fun and moving event.

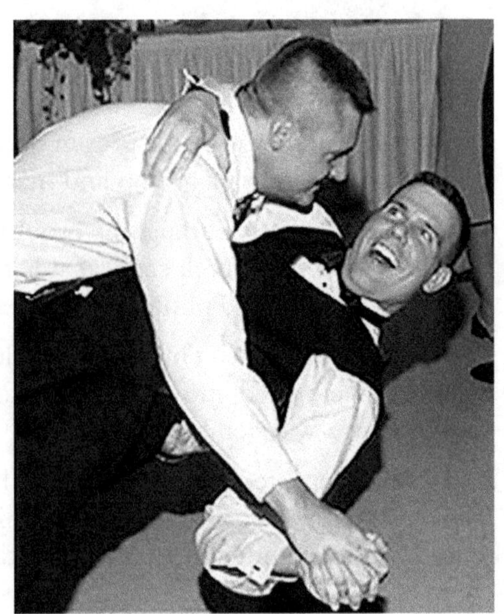

NO, these fellows are not this gay couple mentioned above. I believe one of the guys in that photo is a groom, and the other is just one of the guys in the wedding party. They were just messing around on the dance floor for the fun of it. I think the guy from the wedding party might have been trying to embarrass the groom by dancing with him. I often saw guys tag in on the dollar dance to dance with the groom. They seemed to think it was cute to try to embarrass the groom by dancing with him.

The dollar dance may not be popular all over the country, so I will explain it for those who are not familiar with the tradition.

In the dollar dance, the bride dances with all the guys and the groom dances with all the gals over the course of several songs. Everyone who dances with either the bride or groom gives them money for their honeymoon as they tag in to dance with them. Personally, I always thought the idea was a little tacky.

Once, I did a wedding at Perfect North Slopes, a ski resort in Lawrenceburg, Indiana, just west of Cincinnati. The groom worked there as a ski instructor, and I believe the bride may have also been a ski instructor. Nothing like getting married where you work, especially in such a beautiful location!

The most unique barn weddings I have ever done took place at Heartland Barn in West Harrison, Indiana, which is slightly northwest of Cincinnati, Ohio. This wedding site has been in existence for a very long time. The names and marriage dates of all the hundreds and hundreds of couples who had been married in the barn over the years were scrawled across all the inside walls by those couples. Every surface was covered from floor to ceiling. You could almost sense their presence and spirit when you looked around inside.

The groom was from Australia at a summer camp wedding north of Fort Wayne, Indiana. He had been backpacking his way around the world and had happened to stop at the summer camp for underprivileged kids from Fort Wayne. He stayed on for the summer as a volunteer and met his fiancée there. She was a volunteer as well, and a daughter of the man who ran the camp.

The groom's family and friends from Australia – about an entire airplane full – came over to attend the outdoor wedding and reception at the lodge. What was particularly strange to me about this reception was they only played rock music from Australia.

I had never heard any of the songs. They were all Greek to me, but all the younger guests and wedding party members were constantly dancing to them, singing along with them, and they clearly knew all the words to the songs. It really seemed strange to me that their rock music could be so different from our American rock music.

I went outside at one reception to see what was going on, when I noticed almost everyone in the wedding party had mysteriously disappeared. All the guys were lighting up expensive cigars the groom was passing out. The bride happened by just about then, so I had the guys gather in a semi-circle around her. I took their photo, with the bride holding up a lit cigar and the guys puffing away behind her on theirs. Bet she didn't figure on ever having a wedding photo like that one!

Brides who wanted to use city parks for group photos in Indianapolis and Cincinnati had to buy photo permits from the Parks Department, or risk being run off by park rangers. I found out about this requirement after we all got run out of one park in Cincinnati by the park rangers for taking photos without having purchased a park photo permit. It seems they didn't mind us taking photos there, as long as they made money off it. They gave the bride the choice of purchasing a permit on the spot for about $150 or leaving. The bride decided she really didn't want her photos taken there; after all, we were nearly finished with photos when the rangers arrived. A couple of later brides decided to take their chances and do photos without a permit. They were lucky enough not to be caught and chased out of the parks. I always held my breath when they insisted on trying to just get away with it.

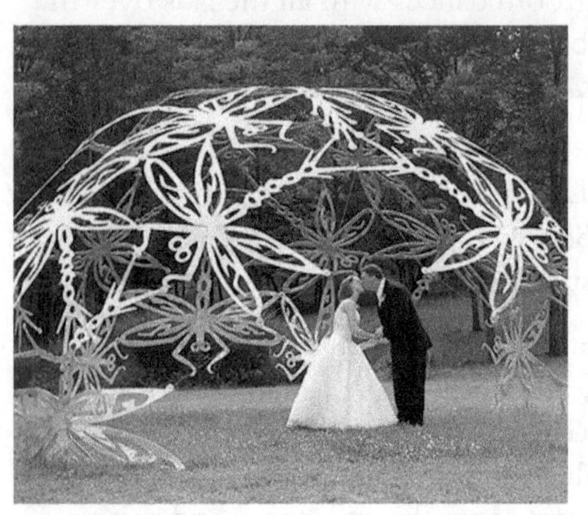

If you are ever in Hamilton, Ohio, try to drive through the Pyramid Sculpture Park there. You might have to pay a slight admission price. It is on the property of a lawyer who supposedly owns about half the buildings in downtown Hamilton – or so I was told.

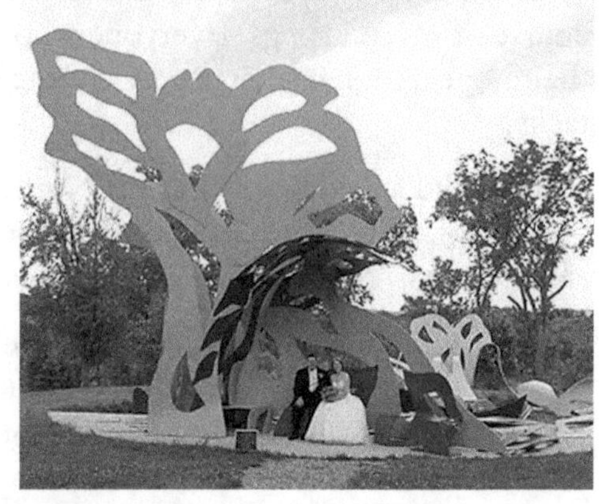

The wealthy lawyer's home is on the property. It is an underground house with a tinted glass pyramid rising out of the ground to a height of maybe twenty feet or so, which serves as a skylight for his home. His underground house has been featured on the TV program "Extreme Homes."

Scattered over several acres on his property, and accessible by roads, are between fifty and one hundred colorful giant sculptures he had commissioned artists to make. Some of these sculptures seem as big as a house. It is a popular spot for weddings and is a photographer's dream, when it comes to unique backgrounds to photograph wedding parties and bridal couples against.

I covered one reception at the Verdin Bell and Clock Museum in downtown Cincinnati. The historical building is the decommissioned 1850 St. Paul's Church, which the Verdin Company purchased for one dollar, with the promise to restore and maintain the building. Restoration ended up taking a couple of years and costing nearly a million and a half dollars in the early 1980's.

It housed an amazing assortment of antique church tower clock mechanisms and church bells that had been cast in sand molds, the old world way, in Verdin Company's foundry in Cincinnati since 1842. It was called a museum back when I covered the reception there. I've noticed they are now calling it Verdin Bell Event Center, and it is still available for private rental. Check out photos of the exquisitely beautiful Verdin Bell Event Center at: http://www.verdin.com/about/bell-event-centre.php.

The most majestic and awe-inspiring church I ever came across in all of my 45 years of photographing weddings was the gigantic, beautiful Catholic Basilica in Covington, Kentucky. If I remember correctly, it had a raised open area in the middle of the church, where the services were held. This gave it the feeling of being a church in the round.

I photographed a couple of after-hours receptions at the Indy Children's Museum. One took place during the huge traveling display of blown glassware by Dale Chihuly. The crowning centerpiece of his display was a multicolored glass sculpture about four stories tall, which colorfully filled the spiraling circular walkway that ran between all the floors of the museum. His glasswork filled the entire museum and made for some interesting photos and backgrounds. I tried to capture it all the for bride, so she would always be able to remember how beautiful her reception site had been on the day of her wedding.

I also did weddings in many famous old mansions in Indianapolis that bore world famous family names like Stokely and Allison.

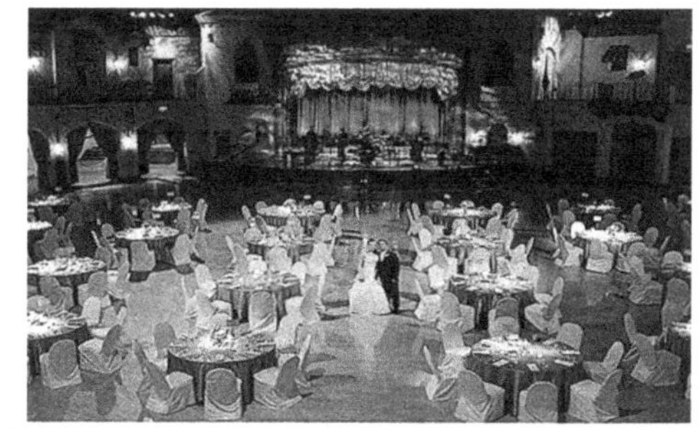

The fabulous Indiana Roof Ballroom was, in my opinion, the most beautiful of all the locations I encountered in my career. It had a beautiful circular ceiling that was painted to resemble a cloud-filled sky. They put on an indoor thunderstorm display, including lightning which was accompanied by the sound of rolling thunder, while the house lights were dimmed. I love the art deco styling of the room, too. The walls of the circular room were made to resemble an Italian villa, with balconies on the second floors of the false building fronts that encircled the room.

In 1963, when I was right out of high school, I went to dances with nationally known rock and roll entertainers at the Indiana Roof Ballroom regularly during the summer. I remember one of the entertainers was the guy who had the hit "Midnight Mary." Being there again to photograph weddings was like a homecoming to me.

I photographed three weddings at the rotunda of the Indiana State House in Indianapolis. The groom in one wedding was an aide to the governor. We were even granted access to the governor's inner office to take some photos. It looks a lot like what I imagine the Oval Office of the White House would look like, with a huge – about eight feet across – Governor of Indiana Seal on the floor in the middle of the room.

The Indiana State House is quite lavish, as politicians have spent lots and lots of the taxpayers' money making it lavish! It used to be available for free, on a first come first serve basis, to any resident of Indiana on Saturdays for their wedding. I believe there is now a token charge to stage a wedding there. It is still first come first serve basis as far as reserving it goes. While it's not free anymore, the token charge is nothing close to the price of renting as nice of a location anywhere else.

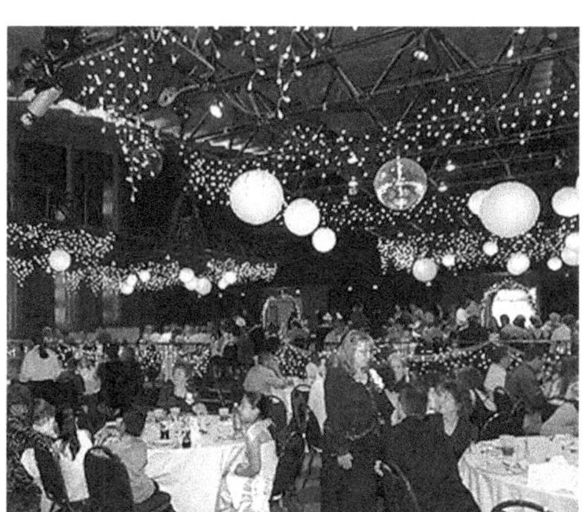

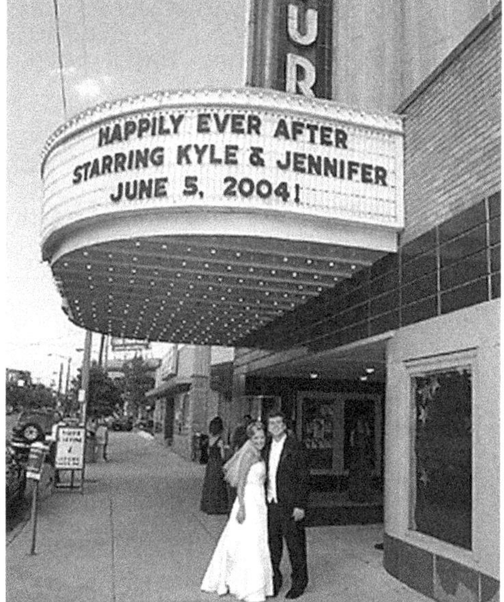

Getting to photograph a lot of really unique and beautiful wedding and reception locations, such as various museums and zoos in Indianapolis, Cincinnati, and Columbus, Ohio, was deeply rewarding. Also among the highlights were the hand-built stone Loveland Castle in Cincinnati, restored art deco big band era dance halls in the Chicago area, and restored art deco 1930's movie theaters in Anderson, Indiana, the Oakley section of Cincinnati, and one in downtown Indianapolis. These photos are of the Oakley 20th Century Theater.

Here is a listing I had posted on unique wedding/reception sites as they appeared on my website:

Most Unique Wedding Locations I've Come Across in the Cincinnati Area:

- Pyramid Hill Sculpture Park in Hamilton, Ohio
- Union Terminal Train Depot and Museum
- Verdin Bell & Clock Museum
- Manor House
- Drees Pavilion at Devou Park
- The 20th Century Theater in Oakley=>
- The Heartland Barn in West Harrison, Indiana
- Tori Station in Fairfield
- Spring Grove Cemetery
- The Phoenix
- Chateau Pomije Winery in Guilford, Indiana
- Cincy Bengals Football Stadium

Most Unique Wedding Locations I've Come Across in the Indianapolis Area:

- Indiana Roof Ballroom in downtown Indy
- White River Gardens at the Indy Zoo
- Indy Children's Museum
- Fountain Square Theater
- Allison Mansion and Stokely Mansion at Marian College
- Hanna House Mansion (supposedly haunted)
- Oak Hill Mansion in Carmel
- Valle Vista Country Club in Greenwood
- Community Life Center at Forest Hills Cemetery
- Indiana State Museum
- Indianapolis Museum of Art
- Lumiere du Corp
- Ritz Charles in Carmel
- Omni Severin Hotel in downtown Indy
- The Republican Club on Monument Circle

Chapter 9: People I've Met

In about 1996, I met a DJ from the Chicago area named Steve Wozniak who worked out of Elkhart, Indiana. He had been hired for a reception in Shelbyville, Indiana for a wedding I did there.

He said he was so impressed with how thorough my coverage was and my technique of displaying photos at the reception on my laptop that he wanted to pitch my services on his website. He told his clients, "Hey! If Bill Collins is available for your wedding date, you just have to hire him. He is the best photographer I've seen in over twenty years of DJ-ing weddings!" During the next year, he was responsible for quite a few brides hiring me for their weddings in both Indianapolis and Chicago.

Steve's DJ-ing skills impressed me as much as my photography skills impressed him. He was the best DJ I had ever seen! He had been a nationally top-rated DJ in California, before moving to the Elkhart, Indiana, area, where he lived while working the Chicago wedding market. He really had the ability to get everyone up, dancing, and enthusiastic about the festivities. He made receptions fun.

Since we worked really well together, I returned the favor and promoted his services on my website, too. Before long, we were running into each other frequently at weddings, both in the greater Chicago and Indianapolis areas. He was getting me business in Chicago, and I was having tons of brides in Indianapolis hire him as their DJ. We seemed to play off of each other's abilities to improve our own parts of the assignments and enjoyed working together.

There was a female minister at a large church on North Meridian Street in Indianapolis who hired me for her own wedding, which took place at her church. Following her wedding, she often recommended me to couples who were getting married at her church.

Caterers, reception hall managers, and wedding coordinators would often ask for my card after they had seen me work receptions, so they could refer clients to me. Impressing other wedding vendors in the area really paid off, because they had contact with a lot of brides I would never have reached on my own. Getting them in my corner paid dividends. If you are just starting out as a wedding photographer, never forget how important it is to make a good impression on everyone, because you never know who could give you an assignment or a referral down the road!

One photographer in Hamilton, Ohio, always had beautifully displayed photos in his studio windows, which I admired when I was driving by on my way home late at night from Cincinnati weddings. His studio had lots of big plate glass windows that ran almost a block long, and he put them to good use advertising his wares.

One time, I passed by during the daytime, so I decided to stop and look inside. I told the receptionist who I was, where I was from, and how much I had always admired his window sample photos. The photographer came out and met me. After learning I was not a competitor, he gladly gave me a complete tour of his studio and showed me all his camera room setups. He took me into his sales area and turned on a giant screen TV (which was unheard of back then) and showed me how he used a machine to show his previews on the TV, right from his negatives without using any printed proofs. It was all set to music to complete the effect. I was wowed.

When I got back to Richmond, I purchased the equipment I would need to do the same thing. I sat a second gigantic TV vertically on its side in my camera room. When I took a photo in my studio, my client saw the lifesize image instantly pop up life-size on my TV.

A lady professional wedding photographer hired me to photograph her wedding a few years ago in Indianapolis. She said she couldn't see any way of doing it herself and still get to enjoy the festivities of her special day. I am just glad she chose me.

Recently, I took another look at some of the wedding photos I have taken over the years. When I began putting this book together, I got to see some from my website again. The photos in the Wedding Photo Gallery are the ones I selected. After seeing them again with a fresh eye, I think I might have been a little too hard on myself about not being creative.

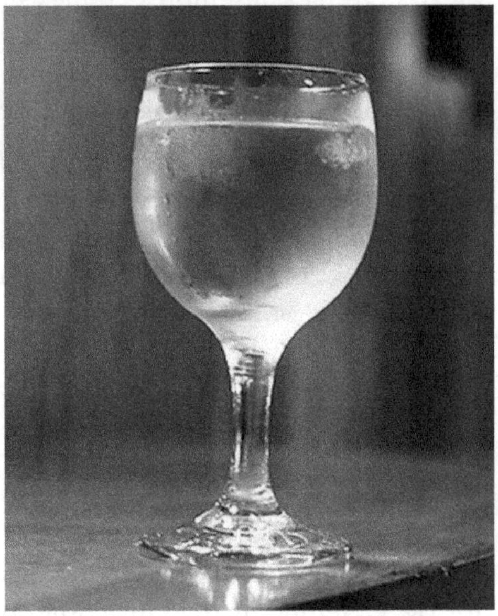

I saw a lot of photos I liked and am proud of having taken, even simple ones like a glass of white wine on a table in a darkened reception hall. I took the photo of the wineglass without flash, and chose a shooting angle which let the light spilling in from an adjacent room paint it from behind. This lighting enabled me to capture the frosty coating on the surface of the glass. Never did a simple glass of wine look as inviting as in this photo!

One of my clients lost her wedding album of 8x10's to a fire. Her insurance company paid for her to get a new album printed, and they paid me the most I've ever been paid. I think it was a couple of thousand dollars or so by the time it was done, as the album she had lost to the fire contained many photographs. She was thrilled with her new album and I appreciated the extra business.

Like most wedding photographers, I always took took great pride in being able to do my job well. I might have even had a tiny bit of an ego when I was younger, but nothing as bad as what I've seen in some other photographers and videographers. I mellowed out and managed to lose any ego I might have had along the way as I got older and wiser.

A lot of my clientele were college students and graduate students. I photographed many weddings at chapels and churches on the campuses of Indiana University, Ohio University, Ohio State University, Purdue University, Notre Dame, Eastern Kentucky University, Miami University in Oxford, Ohio, and Butler University and Marian College in Indianapolis.

Many times, the college fight song of the bride and/or groom would break out among their guests several times during the reception, especially after everyone had had a few drinks. Ohio students liked to use their arms to spell out the letters O-H-I-O over their heads while they sang.

Most people I saw videotaping weddings did so without any professional training. Once, at a local wedding in Richmond, Indiana, a top local Master Photographer showed up with a video camera! I recognized him immediately and didn't know what to think. Maybe he was related to the bride or groom? He knew all the rules photographers work by, but he proceeded to totally ignore them and kept getting in my way at the most inopportune times. Go figure! Maybe he just had a new toy he wanted to play with.

A team of two videographers in Indianapolis used two big television studio quality cameras on tripod dollies. They turned reception sites into their very own TV studio, rolling both their enormous cameras all around the dance floor, getting in the way of the dancing people. Room on the dance floor was always at a premium at receptions, and their two roll-around rigs took up a ton of the available space. They had big lights mounted on both rigs, so no matter where I pointed my camera, it was always facing right into one of their bright lights.

I pulled one of the videographers aside and told him they were breaking one of the cardinal rules of good coverage. by constantly putting themselves into the spotlight and stealing the wedding couple's thunder on their own wedding day. Talk about inflated egos: boy, they had them! They were the stars of the evening, at least in their own eyes.

These inconsiderate videographers never used the zoom feature on their big, expensive studio quality video cameras to shoot from a distance. It would have been simple for them to stay out of everyone's way on the dance floor by using their zoom lens, but they chose to get right up in the dancers' faces and shoot everything at extremely close range.

I have heard how many top photographers spend two or three hours doing group shots. At a wedding photography seminar he was giving, the presenter said he would not even allow himself to be hired unless he was guaranteed at least a full two hours with just the bride and groom, so he could create his masterpieces of the couple.

I never understood why so many photographers took so much time to take group shots, especially considering that after the ceremony all the guests are anxious to eat, drink, and be merry at the reception!

At Valle Vista Country Club in Greenwood, Indiana, just south of Indianapolis, I had a chance to observe this tendency of wedding photographers first-hand. On any summer Saturday, there might be half a dozen weddings and receptions in progress at the same time at Valle Vista Country Club. During my downtime, while everyone ate their meals, I could see other photographers leading various groups of wedding parties about the grounds for photos.

The photographers I remember the most from there was a team of three ladies, who spent twenty minutes alone with just the bride at the gazebo, repeatedly photographing her as she leaned her forearms against the railing. Ten minutes later, the three lady photographers had easily taken a couple hundred nearly identical photos of her in this position from three different camera angles.

I couldn't see the sense for this. The only reason I could see was that they might be trying to make the bride feel like a "star" and the center of attention, giving her fifteen minutes of paparazzi fame on her wedding day. I remember none of these three ladies dressed up in any way for their wedding assignments. They all wore dark slacks with white blouses and flats. In my mind I equated this kind of dress to be like a male photographer showing up in casual dress, without a suit and tie.

In my final few years in the business, the Valle Vista Country Club in Greenwood seemed to have become my home away from home, as I photographed a wedding there, on average, every other weekend during the spring and summer months. I still remember the groom at one wedding there who got weak in the knees, fainted during the service, and had to be revived with smelling salts before the ceremony could continue.

I enjoyed getting paid to be at the biggest and best parties in town, which took place at the swankiest and ritziest places. I really enjoyed my surroundings and the ever-festive atmosphere of the day. I thought I had it made when I finally started becoming fully booked for the year in the big city markets. Who wouldn't like to have a job that only requires you to work one day per week and that pays handsomely? It's impossible not to enjoy your job when everyone around you is always having fun!

A lot of studio photographers have told me they did not enjoy doing weddings, but studio photography did not provide a sufficient income by itself, so they had to supplement with wedding photography. I'm thankful I never had that problem. I loved weddings, and turned each assignment into a challenge to see how thoroughly I could photograph it, which made it fun for me and eliminated any potential burnout.

I had just gone digital with my wedding coverage. I used my Hasselblad film camera equipment to equip a second wedding photographer I had just taken on as an employee, so I could book double and try to increase my income. Let's just call him Mr. Q.

I gave Mr. Q my master pose list and asked him to learn it inside and out, to ensure his coverage was as thorough as my own, without missing any important photos that should be taken at every wedding.

Mr. Q accompanied me to about a dozen weddings, shooting second camera to gain some experience while I trained him.

He showed some promise and eventually improved enough for me to allow him to photograph weddings on his own for me. He would do a decent job on a couple of weddings, then fall apart on the next few, missing several group photos he should have taken automatically. I received complaints from clients.

Like most newbie photographers, Mr. Q stood way too far back from the groups while he was photographing them. I critiqued his images after each wedding he photographed. I usually told him he needed to be closer to his subjects, so the group took up nearly the entire image. Mr. Q's rookie mistake is a common one, and wedding photographers can improve their technique by cropping in tight, so the image fills up the frame with only what you want the finished photo to contain. The bigger your main subject, the better your photo's quality will be.

Like I told Mr. Q, it is all about consistency. He absolutely had to deliver an excellent product at every single wedding, but all Mr. Q ever wanted to talk about was when I would start paying him more money. I think I was paying him around $200 to $300 per wedding. All he had to do was show up with my equipment and take the photos! I booked the dates, I interacted with the client, and I prepared and delivered the final product. I also critiqued his work after every wedding, teaching him how to grow into a better photographer.

When Mr. Q applied for employment with me, I had made it clear to him almost all of the weddings would be in Indianapolis, Cincinnati, and Dayton, Ohio. He said he was fine with traveling to the weddings. I told him I didn't charge my clients mileage, as I did not believe in trying to fleece my clients with added costs. I expected him to buy his own gas, as I felt I was paying him quite well for the hours he was working, especially considering I was also training and educating him. I believe he said he worked a factory job during the week.

At the time he was hired, he had no objections to our arrangement, but after doing just a few weddings on his own, he kept asking to be paid more and more per wedding and to be compensated for mileage. By the time I filled the bride's package, paid for the film and the paper preview prints, and paid Mr. Q, I wasn't making much more than he was, even though I was double-booking assignments. Back then, I think I was charging $995 or $1,095 for my top package, and I also had the expense of advertising and the studio's overhead costs to cover.

Though I wasn't crazy about it, I finally gave in to Mr. Q and told all the brides they would have to add Mr. Q's gas mileage charges to their package prices if they wanted him to do their wedding.

He never really achieved the consistency I felt was needed to keep my customers happy, so he never got his pay raise. His focus on money rather than the craft of photography led to us parting ways, and I gave up on the idea of training a second photographer.

Mr. Q surely left my employ a much better wedding photographer than he was when I met him, as I had done my best to train him well. I'm not positive that after leaving he didn't become a competitor, but I think he was more likely to have tried to work in the local market rural western Ohio rather than try to succeed in the big city markets I was working.

My encounter with Mr. Q totally soured me on the idea of ever becoming a multiple photographer operation again. Had double booking worked out using Mr. Q, I might have ended up with three or four other photographers working for me, which would have greatly boosted my annual income. I sure had the leads to keep three or four other photographers busy.

I learned early on in my career to always take my own supper meal with me to receptions. Sometimes my clients would invite me to eat, but you would be surprised how many times they wouldn't. Oftentimes, annoyingly, people would wait to ask me to eat until I didn't have time to do so, because the festivities were starting and I had to get back to work.

Usually I purchased a pizza or Subway sandwich on my way to the wedding. During their supper hour, I would slip out to my car to eat, while the guests enjoyed their banquet inside. I started telling my clients that I did not expect them to feed me.

At a reception in either Marion or Anderson, Indiana, the hotel started setting up a beautiful buffet spread in the public space outside the ballroom. I photographed every item on the spread, so the bride could always remember what they had to eat at their reception.

The hotel had also set up a bar. I was extremely thirsty and wanted a Diet Coca-Cola, so I joined the long line, still holding my camera in one hand. It took an unusually long time for me to get through the line and be able to order my drink. As soon as I was handed my Diet Coke, a uniformed security guard standing there told me bluntly I could not have it, as this bar and buffet was for another reception, which would be starting shortly.

I replied that I hadn't realized it wasn't my party's buffet. I told the security guard how long I had been working nonstop, and that I was extremely thirsty and would like to go ahead and buy the Coke, if I could. He still said no. I had to put up with being thirsty for the rest of the night! I had never had a hosting hotel treat me so badly. Usually they bent over backwards to make me feel welcome.

Eventually I found out the wedding couple who had hired me had wanted to have their reception at this ultra-swanky hotel, but didn't want to use their catering services. The hotel would not allow the couple to bring in their own caterer, as they wanted the money from catering it themselves.

The couple ultimately decided to go ahead and use the hotel's catering, but bought the smallest spread available, which must have angered the hotel management. So the hotel put a security guard on duty by the buffet and bar to make sure guests from our reception didn't stray over to the expensive buffet spread and bar.

When the buffet for my couple was uncovered, I started photographing each item as I normally would, and I was shocked by the tiny amounts of food! There were meatballs in one serving dish, but only about a dozen in total. It looked almost completely empty! The rest of the buffet line was equally sparse.

My clients had about a hundred guests, so it didn't take long for the food to run out completely. Most guests went unfed and with nothing to drink for the rest of the reception. I didn't figure out what had happened until later on, and I felt so badly for the couple when I found out.

Later in the evening, I approached the bartender at the other reception's bar again, to ask if there was any other place in the hotel where I could slip away to purchase something to drink. The security guard saw me back at the "wrong bar" and came running up to me, yelling at me that I had no business being there. He was very rude. I told him why I was there, simply to ask if there was somewhere else in the hotel to buy something to drink. He yelled in reply, "Maybe your wedding couple should not have been such tight wads in buying their buffet, and maybe you should go tell them so!" He really created a scene. I told him he was being "an absolute a-- hole" and should be ashamed of himself for attacking me, when all I was trying to do was find out where I could go in the hotel to buy a Diet Coke.

Some of the meals at receptions I have attended would have cost from $35 to $50 – sometimes even more – per guest before 2000. One time, before I started taking my own food to my assignments, I had one wedding coordinator in Cincinnati tell me I would be provided a "bandwich" instead of a meal. A "bandwich" is a perfunctory meal they give band members and other people at weddings who aren't considered guests.

The hotel served all the guests their meals before setting up a tiny table in the kitchen for the DJ and me to eat our bandwiches on. Mine was a chicken salad sandwich, which happened to be one of the best sandwiches I have ever eaten. It was absolutely delicious, but I had to gobble down my bandwich, because getting fed after everyone else had made us rushed to eat and get back to work.

Upon booking a wedding in Northern Indiana, I learned the maid of honor was a young lady who had set a world record in 200-meter freestyle swimming in 2001. I was told she was an Olympic triple gold medalist on the U.S. women's Olympic swimming team. I will refer to her as "Miss O" for Olympian, as I'm sure she would appreciate my being respectful of her privacy.

It was exciting to have the opportunity to meet her. I was amazed by her size. She looked to be well over six feet tall, and her shoulders were a good four feet across and all solid muscle. She seemed very nice but appeared to be an extremely quiet person.

Miss O said she was very impressed by my coverage and the slideshow I put on at the reception. She said she would like me to be the photographer at her wedding, too. I gave her my card and wedding brochure.

Maybe her mother was in charge of hiring the wedding vendors or something, but in any event, I never got the assignment of Miss O's wedding. Then again, Miss O may have simply checked my website and saw I was already booked for her wedding date.

It wouldn't be the first time I had been unavailable for someone's wedding date when I really wanted to photograph their wedding, as was the case in former clients' sibling's weddings. Man, you always hate to turn down repeat business from a family when it comes your way. I never thought to ask Miss O about whether that happened or not.

Several times a bride changed her wedding date just so I could be her photographer. They had contacted me before the date was set in stone, and they volunteered to change it so they could retain my services.

The following year, I was back in that same town in northern Indiana again, only this time it was for Miss O's sister's wedding. Miss O was her sister's matron of honor this time around.

I guess Miss O's --and the bride's-- mother had finally seen my previous work from Miss O's friend's wedding, where Miss O had been the maid of honor, because this time I was hired through an email from their mother with no questions asked.

Miss O's sister had a beautiful ceremony followed by a huge tented outdoor reception at the local country club.

Meeting Miss O twice sure made watching the next summer Olympics a lot more exciting for me, as I got to watch her and root for her in her quest there for more world records and gold medals.

I was disappointed to find out I had not been hired for Miss O's wedding, as I had really been looking forward to it, but I guess you can't book them all.

Professional athletes popped up at weddings a few more times during my career. At a reception in my hometown of Connersville, Indiana, I spied a beautifully stunning lady and asked her if she was a professional model. "Yes," she said, "in New York City." She had come to the wedding with Broadway Joe Namath's backup quarterback for the New York Jets.

At a reception in Columbus, Ohio, I overheard some guests discussing the father of the bride and learned he was a retired Major League Baseball player. Looking over my records, I am lead to believe he was Jim Bruske, a pitcher who played for the Dodgers/Padres/Brewers/Yankees 1995-2000. The same thing happened at a luxury hotel wedding in Cincinnati, where I heard the bride's father was a retired starting pitcher for the Cincinnati Reds.

One of my weddings took place at the Cincinnati Bengals football stadium. We were guided through the belly of the stadium under the grandstands, and were even allowed onto the playing field itself for the group photos.

The stadium staff made all the women go barefoot before allowing them onto the playing surface. Back then, there was a big Bengal tiger painted on the fifty-yard line which made a fabulous foreground object for the group photos. All the guys in the wedding party pretended they were going out for passes, hollering and whooping it up at their chance to be on the Bengals field. Their antics made for some unique and great simulated action photos. I even lined up the girls facing the guys, like two football teams ready for a ball snap for a couple photos. A good time was had by all!

They say imitation is the greatest form of flattery, but boy was I surprised when a photographer out in California emailed me to ask if I knew someone had hijacked my website, proweddingphotos.com, in its entirety – they had changed the name and phone number and reposted the whole site, claiming all of the content as their own!

In response to his email, I Googled some unique language from my website and found both my website and the imitation site in the first couple of listings! It was hard to believe someone would have the nerve to even consider stealing my entire website and claiming it as their own! proweddingphotos.com was copyrighted on every page of the site, so I had a legal basis for complaint as well as an ethical one. I had years of work invested in it.

I contacted the site's owner and told them who I was. I emphasized that my site was totally copyrighted and insisted they take their website down immediately. It was gone by the end of the following day, although the transgressor never returned my email. Unbelievable!

My website is no longer online, but most of it can still be viewed, thanks to Archive.org's Way Back Machine. Click on or copy and paste the following link into your web browser: *https://web.archive.org/web/20100328053954/http://www.proweddingphotos.com/* to see what proweddingphotos.com looked like when it was last actively online.

Chapter 10: To Small Claims Court We Go

In film shooting days, I always prepared a preview album of all the photos, so the bridal couple could select the photos they wanted in their final album as 8x10's. I gave 8x10's because the bigger the print, the better good photography looks -- and it added extra value to my package.

The preview album was signed out for a specific period, then it was to be returned with their choices made. The album of previews was the property of the studio. It was offered as an add-on, should the couple wish to purchase it.

There was a bold faced larger type faced provision in my lawyer-created Wedding Photo Agreement, which imposed a $200 late order fee upon anyone who did not return the previews and place their album order within 6 months after their wedding. It also released me from any responsibility to have to fill any part of their order before the late order fee had been paid, once it had kicked in.

This was included because I did not want anyone to ever again come back five years after their wedding to get their album of prints ordered after the costs to print it had increased. Yes, one bride really did that to me. Also, at the time I had the contract written, I didn't collect their wedding balance until their album order was placed. I soon changed their balance due date to 30 days before their scheduled wedding date, so I didn't have to try to collect on weddings which fell through at the last minute or after brides went broke overspending with other wedding vendors.

Back then, about a fourth of the brides ended up never even placing an order for their finished album of 36 8x10's, preferring to keep their preview albums with 5x5's of all their photos instead. If they had paid their balance, I never complained when that happened, as it saved me the added cost and work of making their finished album.

I had to sue one couple to get paid their balance and get the preview album back. I had called them several times, long distance from Connersville to Richmond, but they would not deal with me, so I took them to small claims court to get it settled.

The groom tried to defend his actions with saying money was tight and I had never attempted to contact them to get the preview album back.

The case went my way when I was able to produce my long distance telephone bills with their phone number on it numerous times, along with how many minutes the conversations had lasted on each of those calls. "Having proven he lied once, none of his testimony can be trusted," I argued, and won.

One family hired me for their daughter's wedding. A month before the wedding, the dad calls saying the wedding isn't going to happen because of the groom cheating on his daughter. "My other daughter is getting married in about six months, can we just switch everything over to her wedding?"

Had I turned other brides away for his first daughter's wedding date during the time they had the date reserved? Nobody knew, but it was much too late to hope the date would fill on my schedule. There are only so many prime Saturdays during the spring and summer. Now I had one less. They still owed me about a $600 balance on the first daughter's wedding.

Their second daughter's wedding was during the slower winter season, so I said I would allow it. He called back about two months before his second daughter's wedding, saying her wedding had to be postponed for three months, could we move the wedding date back? I said I would move it to the new date, provided their wedding package balance was paid right now.

Already two wedding dates were lost, I told him, without producing any meaningful income, so he needed to pay me the balance before I would reschedule. Smart move; they sent me the balance, only to call me a month later to tell me the second daughter's wedding was now canceled, too. Could he get his money back? I got paid for a wedding I didn't photograph, but I figure I lost two opportunities to generate income.

The next time someone wanted to un-hire me, I knew better how to handle it. A Bloomington, Indiana groom wanted a refund because their wedding had been canceled. I told him a refund wasn't possible and the contract he and his fiancée had signed was written as a sale; they were on the hook for the balance and would have to pay it, whether I photographed their wedding or not.

He did an immediate about face, saying, "Okay, since we are going to have to pay you anyway, then we want you to go ahead and photograph our wedding as planned!" He had lied about it having been canceled.

Their wedding was photographed just like anyone else's. I treated them as I would any other couple, being nice, polite and doing as thorough of job as I possibly could. Everything was top notch and could not have been done better by anyone else, IMHO.

The groom was mad over not being able to dump me before the wedding. He hid his anger on the wedding day, but afterwards he griped about everything, and even went so far as to post a bad review about my services on an online wedding vendor website.

Finally, I just told him, "Look, every once in a decade or so, photographers run across someone who absolutely refuses to allow you to satisfy them in any way, no matter how hard you try. You are one of those persons. I'm sorry you refuse to allow me to satisfy you in any way."

I will relate this next anecdote to you by stating it involves the proceedings of the small claims court trial in which I was involved. It is not slanderous, because I am relating just my belief of what happened and facts which are substantiated by the court record, which is a matter of public knowledge and legally indisputable. Here was the situation:

The standing seam metal roof on my studio building, which measured approximately 35'x80', was becoming dilapidated. It was badly rusted, and the paint was cracked to the point that it was standing proud of the roof surface. The roof was in desperate need of repainting. I contacted a painting company and dealt with the owner, who we will call Mr. Z to protect his anonymity.

I included specific clauses in the contract, stating my expectations for the job, and also stipulating the job would be done exactly the way I had requested: the roof rust and raised paint would be sanded smooth, then a primer coat would be applied, followed by a final coat of top-quality metal roof paint. I agreed to pay Mr. Z approximately $1,700 if the painting was done precisely according to the specifications included in the contract (this was a long time ago, so $1,700 then would be worth more nowadays).

Mr. Z agreed to all the terms and prices specified in the contract, and we both signed the bid agreement. A week or so later, on a Wednesday (my studio was always closed on Wednesdays), I happened to drive by the studio mid-morning and was shocked to see Mr. Z's paint crew on my roof, rolling paint directly onto the roof without bothering to sand the rust and flaked paint off or apply primer first!

I stopped the car and demanded to know exactly what he thought he was doing. I believe he knew I had caught him red-handed cutting corners on the job. I went inside my studio and fetched my camera while Mr. Z followed me, asking what I was doing. I told him I was going to go outside on the roof and take pictures as evidence of his breach of contract.

He angrily said, "No you're not!" I started around him, when suddenly he belly-bucked me two or three times right there in the reception area of my own studio, attempting forcibly to keep me inside to prevent me from photographing his shoddy handiwork.

I pushed past him without saying anything, went outside, and started heading towards the roof. He called his crew down off the roof and they all quickly disappeared, never to return to my studio to finish the roofing job.

Another painting company had to be hired to finish the job, and Mr. Z and I sued each other in small claims court.

I believed I had an airtight, slam dunk case, as Mr. Z had agreed in writing to do the job a certain way for a certain price and had chosen not to do the job that way when he thought I wouldn't be around to know the difference.

The judge asked Mr. Z when he had planned to do the sanding on the roof, as he had agreed to do in the bid. Mr. Z replied he was going to sand any raised paint after the first coat of paint had been applied. My jaw dropped when the judge seemed to feel this answer was good enough. That was the total extent of the judge's questioning of Mr. Z!

I, on the other hand, was put on the defense by the judge for what seemed like quite some time. The judge seemed upset I had done my best to make the public aware of what had happened, and wanted me to defend my actions, as though I was defaming Mr. Z without cause.

The judge said he would decide the case and advise us of his findings via mail in a few weeks. He looked at me and said he would have to decide if it was in fact me who had breached the contract by not allowing Mr. Z to come back and finish the job.

Apparently, the fact Mr. Z had breached the signed contract first (in my opinion) and the fact he had never expressed any desire to return and finish the job meant nothing to the judge. I'm not certain whether or not I had remembered to make a point of the fact I had not barred Mr. Z from returning to the studio roof to make things right.

The wild spin the judge was putting on all this concerned me and gave me a very bad feeling about my chances of winning. The judge seemed unduly fixated on the fact I had posted about this incident on the internet, too, as though me mentioning the incident online – and, let us be clear, leaving someone a bad review on the internet is by no means illegal – had justified anything Mr. Z had done. I simply replied, "The truth will set me free."

I was suing Mr. Z for enough money to pay the difference the second painter had charged me to correct Mr. Z's botched job. Since I believed I had been defrauded, I may have even sued for triple damages. I might even have sued for the entire amount I had to pay the second painter. Mr. Z, I believe, sued for full payment.

When the ruling arrived in the mail, it said Mr. Z had been awarded something like $100. I was awarded nothing and I was ordered to pay court costs. I believe this small amount was awarded to Mr. Z because the judge felt I would not challenge such a small award. So much for justice, I guess. I personally believe the judge ruled the way he did in order to keep from tarnishing Mr. Z's reputation in the local market.

Before this biased experience in court, I had never had reason to wonder whether Richmond, Indiana was one of those small towns where everything is controlled by a small clique, like an oligarchy, of local politicians and the town's wealthier citizens. I didn't want my small town to be one where someone could make any problem go away if they were well-connected to the local elite.

If I am going to tell you all about my career, I should at least mention the "Bride from Hell" who tried to sue me in small claims court, also in Richmond, Indiana. I have tried to put the experience behind me and forget as much about my encounter with her as possible, but I will do my best to recount what transpired. As with the story about Mr. Z, I am telling this tale from my perspective and based on the court proceedings.

There was nothing unusual or objectionable about my dealings with her until I showed up at the church on her wedding day. The sky was pouring rain in a cloudburst. When I was about a block from the church, I saw a guy hurrying down the sidewalk, getting drenched without an umbrella. I pulled over and shouted to him, asking if he was looking for the wedding. He said he was. I told him he had to turn around; the church was a city block in the opposite direction. He thanked me. I parked the car, got my equipment inside, and set it up.

I went to the basement of the church to take photos of the bride and her bridesmaids getting ready. What I found in the basement was a person holding an enormous camera rig which made my pro rig look puny in comparison. I knew he was most likely a professional photographer or a pro wannabe. I nodded. He nodded back.

I knocked on the door jamb of the room where the girls were getting ready. There was no door on the room, only a drape pulled across the doorway. I told them I was ready for photos as soon as they were.

I took a seat next to the other photographer to wait for the girls to be ready for photos. I commented on what a nice camera rig he had. He responded, "I will be taking photos throughout the wedding and reception". I thought the situation over.

My written contract stated nobody was allowed to shoot my formal group posings without my express consent, as my talent in being able to pleasingly pose groups and move quickly through the group photos was considered a professional skill which was reserved for my benefit alone.

Those formal group photos were also my bread and butter photos, which produced a large portion of the revenue from reprint orders. Master Photographers taught me I should protect my formal group poses. This was a common practice at the time among professional wedding photographers.

Some of the teaching Master Photographers told me they protected their group photo revenue by simply telling their clients they couldn't shoot flash. It would set off their flash units, drain their batteries, and cause them to miss the expressions they were going for in their photos for the bride.

Other pros said they protected their group poses by making everyone sit as a group at the very back of the church until they were called forward to be in a group. They would send the people to the back of the church again when they were no longer needed for the photos. Anyone trying to take group photos from way in the back of the church would end up with a photo interrupted by the pro photographer standing in the middle of it, ruining their shot.

While waiting outside the girls' dressing room in the basement of the church that day, I mulled it over and decided it would be best to inform the other photographer of my exclusivity policy now, to avoid the rather awkward possibility of having to cut him off later in the midst of a group photo session. I figured he was probably someone the bride had hired to photograph her wedding in addition to me, who would probably sell her his group photos cheaply. Either that, or he was someone who had talked the bride into allowing him to take photos, possibly for his sample photo album. I had never seen him before, and thought perhaps he was someone who was just beginning a career in wedding photography or was an aspiring amateur. He didn't seem upset when I told him about my contract and explained he would not be allowed to photograph my formal group setups. He just nodded and went on his way.

Then, something quite strange happened. The bride and her bridesmaids refused to come out of the dressing room for photos and also wouldn't allow me in. I knocked and asked if they were ready every ten minutes or so, and the bride would always answer they weren't ready yet. The last few times I asked, the curtain on the door was pulled back, and I could see them just sitting there, doing nothing, but they still mysteriously wouldn't move or come forward for photos. It finally dawned on me they had been able to hear every word I had said to the other photographer.

We were running out of time, as the wedding was scheduled to begin very soon. The girls finally came out, but with hardly any time left to take photos. I was really under time pressure even to get the amount of photos I did. There was a downstairs stage at hand with a solid–color, full-length curtain which made a decent background. It was too late to take them upstairs, as most of the guests were already seated in the pews by now. I only had a few seconds to arrange each group and really felt rushed. I did the best I could under the time constraints I found myself in, but would have greatly preferred to have had more time.

The bride's parents appeared, and I quickly took photos of the bride with them. It turned out the guy I had met outside who was getting soaked in the rain was the bride's father. The shoulders of his coat showed the effects of having been rained on.

Time was up. It was time for the wedding to begin. I barely had time to scurry upstairs and get into position to record the processional. The ceremony was uneventful, but as soon as I started doing formal group photos, I saw the photographer I had encountered downstairs flop down in an aisle seat about three rows back.

Every time I posed a group, I could hear his camera shutter click behind me. After about the fourth time I heard him copying my poses, I told him he could not continue photographing the groups I was posing. I told him that he could feel free to put together and photograph any groups he wished after I was finished. I was firm in my pronouncement, but tried to be nice and courteous at the same time.

My kind but strict request was not effective; he continued to shoot every group I posed from behind me. Finally, I drew the line, saying, "If I hear your camera shutter click again, even just once more, I am done here. I'll consider my contract, which says you can't knock off all my posed formal groups, as breached, and will leave without finishing my job."

The bride, groom, nor anyone else at the wedding spoke up to back me up on my rights the signed contract reserved exclusively for me. Nothing at all was said by anyone. Our wedding photo contract stated that in situations such as this one, the bride and groom had the responsibility to intercede on my behalf and defend my exclusive rights to photograph the formal groups I posed. No such luck.

My point had found the mark. The other photographer finally turned off his camera and put it away. The rest of the day proceeded smoothly without further incident. A month or so later, I was served with a notice stating I was being sued by that bride in small claims court in Richmond.

At the hearing, she tried to blame me for everything imaginable that went wrong at her wedding. I was supposedly responsible for her father's suit being wet from the rain in the photos; I was responsible for the group photos of the girls taken in front of the basement stage curtain being less than perfectly posed; I was responsible for there being electrical outlets showing on the wall in one photo; etc. She even claimed I didn't have exclusive rights to photograph her wedding. She alleged I had ruined her wedding by calling out the other photographer and making him stop taking the formal groups I had posed.

In reply to these charges, I explained to the court that her dad's coat would have been even wetter if I hadn't steered him in the direction of the church prior to the wedding. I defended how rushed I was to take the photos by the time the girls came out of the dressing room, and how they had just sat in the room and refused to move until the very last minute.

I produced the signed wedding photo contract and explained the contract reserved all photography rights for the formal groups I posed exclusively for me, and that by signing it, the bride and groom had agreed to abide by my terms and conditions, but had failed to do so.

Much to the bride's dismay, her case against me was promptly thrown out of court. She huffed. She puffed. She fumed. She stormed out of the courtroom. I thought the petty issue was finally over, but about six weeks later I was served notice she was suing me again in small claims court. I didn't know what to think.

As soon as the judge saw both of us before him again, he tore into the bride. He told her the issue had been decided at the last hearing, and just because she didn't like his ruling, she didn't get to take two bites at the apple and bring suit over it again. He ran her out of his court and apologized to me for being dragged into court twice over the same issues.

While on the subject of contracts and such, let me say I learned from all these encounters and evolved my business practices accordingly. I raised my prices and changed my pricing arrangements and started collecting the balance for covering a wedding paid in full at least thirty days prior to the wedding date.

With my higher prices, I no longer had to rely on reprint orders for a major part of my wedding income, so I dropped the clause in my contract about reserving the rights to my formal group setups and welcomed others to take group photos, too. Doing so allowed me to really be "Mr. Nice Guy," since I didn't have to protect my reprint order income anymore.

Surprisingly, the worst I was ever treated by a wedding party was at a wedding I did for an extremely close relative when he got married. I think his family thought I was simply going to give them my services and an album of photos as my wedding gift, free of charge.

I might have, too, except these relatives had always thought of me and treated me as the "family screw-up", all the way from my teen years into my early forties. I was book-smart, having skipped a year in high school and graduating with 54 college prep credits when only 32 were needed, but not nearly as intelligent as my two ingenious older brothers who had great careers after graduating college.

I did seem to lack any common sense until after marrying my wife, Sue, when I was in my early forties. Sue finally instilled some common sense into me.

By then I was a full-time professional photographer and studio owner. I wanted my family members to show me a little bit of respect, for a change.

I told the groom's mother we would be purchasing a gift of our choosing as his wedding present, but I would not be covering his wedding for free. I was available to photograph his wedding, since I would be in attendance, but they would have to hire and pay me just like any other customer.

This news didn't seem to sit too well with them. They said they wanted me as photographer, but were reluctant to send in their retainer fee. They delayed so long in sending it in that finally I threatened to open the date back up to anyone else who was willing to pay my retainer if they weren't willing to lock it down.

Ultimately, I was hired and did my close relative's wedding. I was still shooting medium-format film back then with my Hasselblad cameras. I doubled the amount of photos I normally took at a wedding at no added charge to do as thorough a job as possible for them, as I wanted to be sure to please.

He must have complained to his friends in the wedding party about having to pay me, because all night long everyone in the wedding party, people I did not even know, continually made snide remarks to me when I was in their vicinity. They did the same thing to my wife. She asked me why everyone was treating us so badly, and was upset and hurt over it.

The one time I tried to take a few minutes off for one dance with my wife, wedding party members came and got me a minute or so into our dance, saying there were more wedding party photos which needed to be taken right then. I had taken tons earlier, but went along with their request.

There wasn't much we could do but endure the reception until it was over. It wasn't pleasant, but we got through it. I don't know if someone put them up to doing this to us, or whether it was something they decided to do on their own. I am pretty sure we have not seen that relative since his wedding, which must have been twenty or so years ago. Enough said.

Chapter 11: Was I a Klutz?

At the Leland Hotel Ballroom in Richmond, Indiana, I was on the raised stage with footlights recessed on a slant along the very front of the stage. My Hasselblad camera rig was heavy. I had it up to my eye, looking for photos to capture. With so much weight being held so high, I was top heavy but didn't know it.

When I took a little step forwards without realizing where I was standing, my foot hit the slanted footlight recess and I found myself being immediately catapulted forward. Off the stage I went, onto the dance floor among the dancers. I somehow managed to turn sideways during my fall and get the camera away from my face and out from underneath me. I was lucky not to damage it.

The music stopped, and suddenly there was a swarm of people surrounding me. I started to get up, but one guy pushed down on me and told me not to get up because I might be injured. I was told not to move until a medic had checked me out.

A short time later, an ambulance crew arrived and removed me to a smaller connecting room where I was quickly checked over and advised to go to the hospital for further examination. I told them, "No, I'm OK. I won't go with you to the hospital. I have an assignment to complete." They finally gave up, told me to go to the emergency room if I started feeling faint, and left.

I went back into the ballroom to continue my coverage. I felt embarrassed and conspicuous, because I had stolen the spotlight and interrupted the festivities. To my surprise, everyone in the ballroom rose to their feet and gave me a standing ovation.

Back then, photographers traditionally left receptions after the bouquet and garter toss. I had asked the couple if they were ready to do those earlier, but the bride said the groom wanted to hold off for an hour or so, to give the guests something more to look forward to.

If the couple had agreed to do the bouquet and garter tosses when I first suggested, I would have been sitting in an easy chair at home at the time I took my tumble. After I returned to the ballroom from being checked out by the medics, no more time was wasted in getting those last two photos done.

My second wedding-related fall happened at a really swank home, on Geist Reservoir in Indianapolis. We were at the home taking photos prior to traveling to the wedding site. After a lot of indoor photos, I suggested moving outside for some pictures with the reservoir in the background.

We had just started taking group photos when I backed up in an attempt to get everyone into the photo. Everything was fine – and then it suddenly wasn't. I tumbled and fell backwards onto the cover of their in-ground swimming pool, which I didn't even know was there.

Only my pride was hurt. I handed my camera up to someone standing poolside so I could pull myself back up onto the solid cement patio. Miraculously, only about six inches on the elbow of my suit got wet.

Everyone was glad their pool had the canvas cover stretched over it, me most of all! Without it, the water would have ruined my entire camera rig and nice suit. We got back to taking photos without delay.

My third tumble came when I was in Indianapolis for a medieval-themed wedding one wintry Saturday morning. It sure brings back lots of really painful memories to think about it now.

I had covered another wedding in Indianapolis, on Friday night, so I had stayed overnight at a motel on the west side of town, to save myself a trip.

It was extremely cold in Indianapolis, with snow and ice everywhere. I had just finished loading my equipment into my car at the motel the next morning when I suddenly slipped on a patch of black ice next to my car. My feet shot out from under me and I fell backwards, fast and hard. My head snapped back and hit the frozen pavement, and my tailbone took a tremendous jolt.

It seemed like a full two or three minutes passed before I was able to get my breath back. I tried to yell for help, but nobody heard me. Everything around me seemed to be spinning in circles. My head pounded and my tailbone really hurt. I lay there trying to figure out what had happened, hurting and nauseated.

"If I can just manage to get up and get back into my motel room so I can lie on the bed for a minute or two, I will be all right," I told myself. I finally managed to do it, but realized if I continued to lay there, I might be late getting to the church to take the pre-wedding group photos.

With great pain, I lowered my body into the driver's seat of my car and went to the wedding site to set up my equipment. I somehow managed to get through the wedding and reception coverage, even though I was in immense pain.

The medieval-themed wedding was more interesting than most, because the men wore full suits of armor, complete with swords and shields, while the women wore medieval dresses.

I have never been as glad to finish an assignment and get home again as I was after my tumble in the icy parking lot of the motel. I was sore for at least three weeks!

I covered another medieval-themed wedding in full costume at Camp Atterbury, in southern Indiana near Bloomington. It was an outdoor wedding, complete with jesters and medieval musicians. The meal was authentically medieval too: stew served in bread bowls, and meats eaten as finger food.

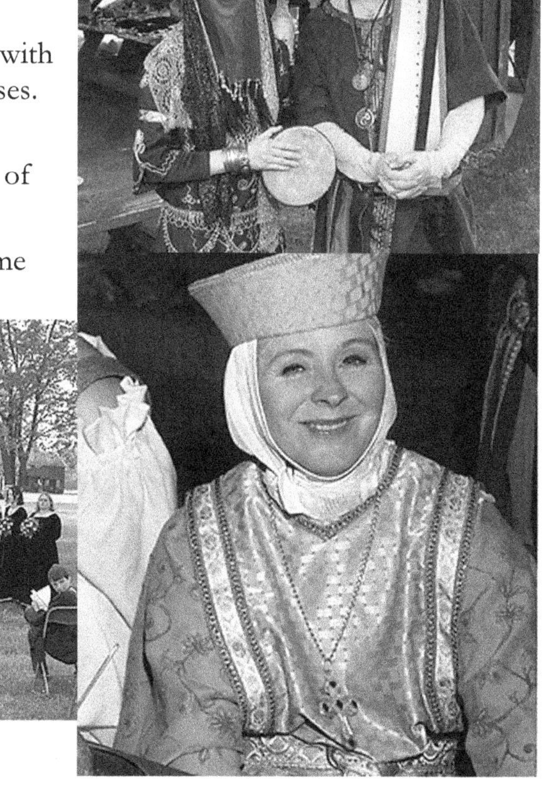

After reading these

three anecdotes about me falling, you may have concluded I was somewhat of a klutz. These three incidents occurred over the span of a 45-year career, and one fall on average every fifteen years isn't so bad!

Having successfully run the Las Vegas Marathon at age 58, I trained hard for over six months the following year to run the Flying Pig Marathon in Cincinnati, Ohio. The race was to start around 7 a.m., so I took a downtown hotel room the night before near the start/finish line.

My alarm went off around 5 a.m. I jumped up and put on my running socks. I then felt the need to use the bathroom. Still not fully awake, I entered the bathroom and immediately slipped on the slick marble floor in my sock feet, going down backwards and cracking my head on the super hard marble floor.

I laid there and ask myself, "What have I gone and done now?"

I got ready and made the start of the race and felt fine for the first six miles. At mile marker 10, I had to stop to upchuck. I was feeling nauseated. I continued on to mile 12, where I had to stop and spend 15 minutes in a porta potty, because I was now suddenly suffering from a really bad case of diarrhea.

I knew I was in no shape to continue the race, so I took a bus for race dropouts back to the finish line. What a disappointment! I would say I probably had received a mild concussion from my bathroom fall

Chapter 12: Things I Saw

I actually decided to write this book because I started having crazy dreams after I had been retired for a few years. These dreams were robbing me of my sleep. They were about things going wrong while photographing weddings that I could do nothing to control. Those things never even came close to having happened when I was actively photographing weddings.

I dreamt about things like being late for a wedding because I wasn't done making my own film to shoot at the wedding! Crazy! I dreamed that I was watching helplessly as a roll of fully exposed medium format film fell from my fingertips at the altar in front of everybody being photographed. Everyone there, including me, watches it unroll down the aisle in front of me, ruining the film and obliterating all the images taken on the roll. Again, totally crazy. I haven't used a roll of film in over twenty years!

I always had feared dropping an exposed roll of film before getting it safely sealed and knew it was a possibility, so I always held all exposed rolls of film very tightly, using both hands until I had licked the attached adhesive strip on the end and sealed the roll with it. I exaggerated this effort.

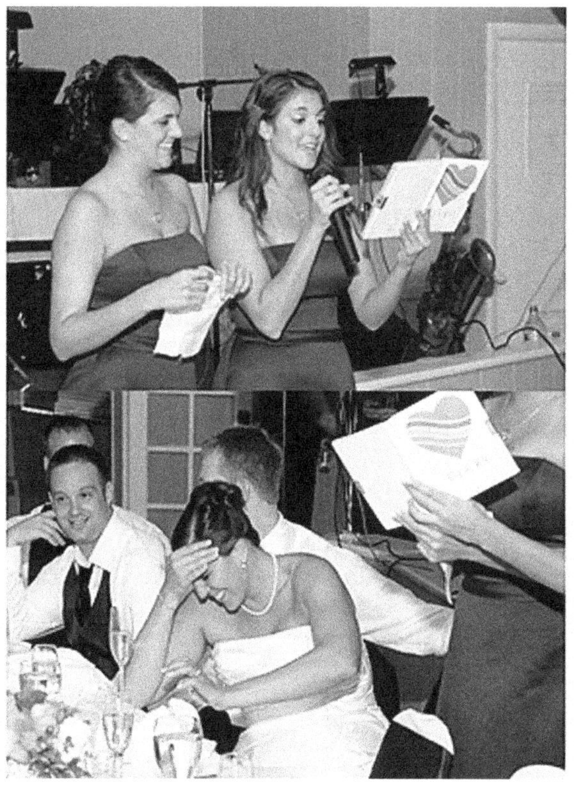

The funniest thing I remember seeing at a reception was when the bride's sister got up to make her wedding toast. She said, "As everyone here knows, the bride was extremely boy-crazy as she grew up." Everybody there laughed a knowing laugh.

She then pulled out the bride's own personal childhood diary and read aloud humorous readings from different bookmarked sections of it for a good fifteen minutes. She told about how hung up the bride had been on different boys she had known and how she had thought this one or that one was so dreamy or good-looking.

Everyone there got a good roaring laugh out of it. It was funnier than most professional stand-up comedians' routines! The bride took it all in stride and seemed to enjoy it as much as anyone there.

The newly married couple arrived at their country club reception site in a horse-drawn carriage, one of those used on Monument Circle in downtown Indianapolis for carriage rides. Seeing a photo opportunity, I had the wedding party line up before going into the reception, using the horse and carriage as a photo backdrop.

Just as I was ready to take the photo, two of the girls in the wedding party let out blood-curdling screams and jumped at least a foot in the air. It turned out they were standing near the business end of the horse when it felt the need to take a whiz.

Those girls, the ones who screamed, had gotten soaked before they even knew what hit them. The horse's whiz had bounced off the concrete, splattering and thoroughly soaking the entire backs of their long gowns. Boy, they were really popular for the rest of the night! Say, does this shoot down my super hero status? I hope not.

While waiting to start formal group photos, a minister made a point of telling me one of his favorite stories. It was about an encounter with a videographer from one of the Dayton, Ohio, television stations who was hired to video a wedding in his church, way back when that wasn't done very much. The minister told him what the rules were for filming his video. The guy responded he was a TV cameraman and knew what to do. There was no need to worry.

The bride and groom were starting to say their vows at floor level, when the minister saw really shocked looks on everyone in the audience. Jaws were dropping open! He turned around to see what was going on.

There was the TV cameraman, perched high above the minister's head with his TV camera balanced upon his shoulder. He was shooting down over the minister's head and shoulders from that vantage point, standing with one foot on top of the pulpit and his other foot on the railing. He was about four feet off the floor, shooting downward.

The minister said he wasted no time running him down from his brazen perch and banished him to the back of the church before continuing with the ceremony. Now that's funny! The minister swears it is true, too!

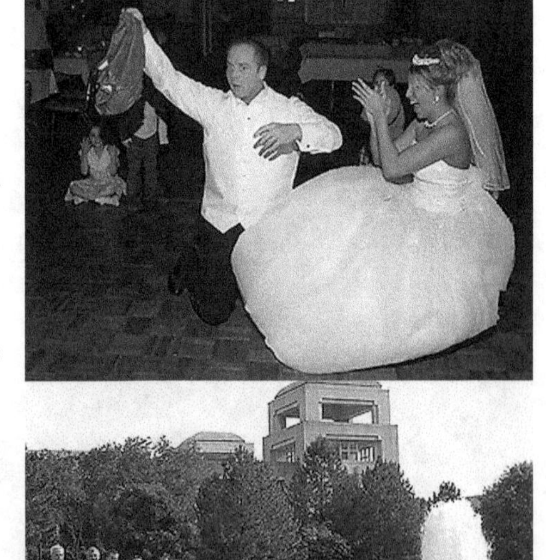

A groom at another wedding clued me in to be ready for something special when he removed his bride's garter at the reception. I was really on my toes and nailed the expression on his face when he came out from under her dress, with a pair of red bloomers which were big enough to fit a full grown elephant! He had such a shocked look on his face as he held them high in the air and stretched them out for everyone to see.

While photographing a huge high-society wedding party at the State Office Buildings in downtown Indianapolis, I had to keep backing up a hill in order to get back far enough to capture the entire wedding party and the water fountain in the photos. I didn't have my wide-angle lens with me during this part of the assignment and had to make do without it.

Suddenly I felt something brush across my shoulders as I backed up. I had run into a row of tall hedges and gotten pretty deep into them before I knew what was happening to me. The real problem was tons of pigeons had been roosting in and on the hedges for ages, and the hedges were totally covered with an overabundance of white bird poop – and now, so were the shoulders of my dark suit jacket.

The rest of the assignment had to be finished without me wearing a jacket, after I showed everyone my coat and explained what had happened to it. Everyone got a laugh out of it and I wasn't penalized for not being formally dressed the rest of the day. After this experience, I kept a spare suit, a spare white shirt, and a couple of spare ties in my car.

Once I saw the ring bearer steal the show. He made a statement he wasn't wild about being ring bearer when he stopped halfway down the aisle, turned, and threw his ring bearer's pillow like a Frisbee towards the back of the church.

During the ceremony, he totally stole the show again when he went up right behind the bride, groom, and minister and sat down on the steps there, facing the audience. He proceeded to stick his finger inside his shirt collar, and he kept tugging at it, trying to stretch his collar out. He made faces, rolled his eyes, stuck out his tongue, while pulling his tie over his head like he was being hanged with it. He brought the entire audience to a roar of laughter. You have to watch those kids. They'll steal the show every time!

The smallest church wedding I ever did involved just me, the minister, and the bride and groom. It can't get any simpler.

At the Rush County Fairground in Rushville, Indiana, about twenty years ago, all the single ladies were lined up for the bouquet toss. One woman, who happened to be wearing a tube top, seemed to really want to be the one to catch it. She out-jumped everyone else, but in the process, her hooters went into motion too. They rose and rose and kept climbing, not stopping until they had seen the light of day. She was even quicker getting her clothing rearranged properly again than she was catching the bouquet! Yes, she caught the bouquet. No, I didn't get the clothing malfunction on film.

During coverage of a wedding at the chapel on Miami University's campus in Oxford, Ohio, just before taking group photos of the men, I glanced toward the rear of the church. The outer doors had been left open to allow air to circulate throughout the building. The step leading up to the chapel door was very low – apparently too low, since a snake had slithered up the step and was making its way toward us down the aisle!

The groom was brave, scooping it up from the floor. The snake wrapped itself around his wrist. He carried the snake outside and released it in the grass. When he returned, I asked him if he had noticed the snake had a diamond pattern on its back. The groom got all pale and seemed a little woozy. It took a couple minutes for the color to return to his cheeks.

Tuxedo rentals were a side line business I had for several years while working the local market in Richmond, Indiana. One bride even put all of her bridesmaids in tuxes for her wedding, just to be different. Boy, talk about being hard to fit for tuxes! Girls are certainly built differently than boys are!

Tuxedo fittings were done at our home back then, as I had not yet bought my studio building. One of the guys who was there for a fitting happened to have been in our basement a few weeks before fixing our furnace or our plumbing. While he was being fitted for his tux, our darkly brindled Persian cat came into the room and he started really laughing hard.

He told us why our cat had made him laugh. On his trip to our basement, he had encountered a pair of large glowing yellow eyes in the dark crawlspace he was in. He said he had been scared half to death and had gotten out of our crawlspace as fast as he could when those eyes appeared. He had just now come to realize that what he had seen in the dark had been our Persian cat.

For my stepson's wedding, his best man had to be replaced with a stand-in when he didn't show up in time for the wedding. My stepson's original choice for best man finally arrived just before the reception ended. He had been involved in a fistfight, and the tux I had rented to him was all torn, bloody, and dirty.

In Plain City, Ohio, the highlight of an Amish bride and groom's entire wedding day was having their photo taken with the full moon rising in the background, and photos of their guests waving lighted sparklers as the newlyweds drove away from the reception in their horse and buggy.

I was surprised to be hired to photograph an Amish wedding, as I had always heard they did not believe in having pictures taken of themselves. I guess all Amish are not the same, or maybe some make exceptions on special occasions. I've also done Mennonite and Quaker weddings, as Richmond, Indiana is a town that was originally settled by Quakers and has a Quaker college.

Some of the best partying down I've ever seen occurred at about a dozen receptions I did late in my career at the Rathskelter, a German restaurant and reception site just north of downtown Indianapolis.

People always loosened up as the evening went by, as they got more liquor in them. Sometimes they got downright plastered by the end of the evening. I remember one shindig at the Rathskelter where, by the end of the night, the bride and her maid of honor were dancing on the tops of the tables they had dined on earlier. I don't think I've seen people have as much fun before or since.

Parking spots were really hard to come by near the Rathskelter. I always had to hunt for one, and sometimes I ended up carrying both of my cameras and my reception equipment bag for a long city block or more.

One night at the Rathskelter, I came out in the wee hours of the morning at the end of the festivities, and went to where I had parked my car. It simply wasn't there. It was gone. There I stood, with all my equipment in hand and no way home. I could not believe this was happening. Had it been stolen or towed? Would I have to call the police or have my wife get out of bed in the middle of the night and drive over sixty miles to come and get me?

I didn't carry a cell phone back then, so I borrowed one from a bouncer at a nearby bar who was manning the entryway to his establishment, after explaining my predicament in detail. Up on the side of the building next to where I had parked was a sign with the phone number of a towing company to call if your car had been removed from the lot. My call to the towing company revealed that they had not towed my car from the lot. I returned the cell phone to the bouncer and considered my options.

There were several streets intersecting each other at odd angles where I parked. Looking around, it dawned on me there were several such tiny triangular lots, all at this same intersection. I hoped that maybe I was simply at the wrong lot! Right across the street, I could suddenly see part of a car parked behind the hedges in the other lot which looked strangely familiar. I crossed the street and was so relieved to find it was my car. I had just been confused about where I had parked it. All of my worries faded quickly as I loaded up my equipment and quickly headed home.

When I was getting ready to park in a field already full of parked cars at an outdoor wedding in rural Ohio, the best man jumped in his car. He threw it into reverse, gunned it, and managed to T-bone my vehicle. "Man, I don't know how that happened, I looked in my mirror before I backed up!" he exclaimed. I replied, "You are supposed to be looking behind you while you are backing up, not just before." Man, what a way to start photographing a wedding!

Once, I arrived at a church in Richmond for a wedding, only to find the church dark and the doors locked. Calling the bride on the phone revealed she had caught her fiancé red-handed in bed with another woman a couple of days before the wedding, so obviously it was a wedding which wasn't going to happen. If only she had called me when she had decided to scrub the wedding, I could have been saved the effort of getting ready and going to the church.

My wife recently reminded me of one time while we were dating when I had to rush off to a wedding, only to realize after it was too late to turn back that I had on my "dress tennis shoes" instead of my dress shoes. I must have looked pretty funny dressed in a formal suit and tennis shoes! I explained what had happened on my arrival and completed the assignment dressed like that. Only now does the thought cross my mind that I could have stopped and quickly bought another pair of dress shoes on the way to the wedding. Hindsight is 20/20!

While stopping to take photos of a wedding party at Soldiers' and Sailors' Monument on Monument Circle in downtown Indianapolis, I came to realize I had locked my keys inside my car with the motor still running. Luckily, I always carried a second set of keys on me, but it took a couple of minutes for it to register that my second set of keys were in my pocket. I had already started to panic by the time I realized it. Another close call avoided.

Once, I got to a local wedding in Richmond, Indiana, before realizing I had forgotten to grab a certain piece of camera equipment from my studio. I called my wife to see if she could fetch it for me and bring it to the wedding site so I could keep working in the meantime.

My wife still reminds me that she was cleaning the oven when I called. She wasn't dressed to be seen in public, but she ran the errand for me anyway. I learned to always check that I had all my equipment together the day before a wedding to make sure all was ready.

If I had been at a wedding a couple of hundred miles away from home, I would have just been stuck trying to complete the assignment as best I could. I never again had to worry about having to face this situation, because of the checklist and my prep the day before each wedding.

Couples have hired me and paid my full price just to photograph their receptions, as they had gotten married at distant “destination wedding locations" weeks before and were now celebrating their marriage back home with their families and friends.

The owner of the largest furniture store in our area hired me to photograph his daughter's wedding several years ago in the backyard of their home. The star of the day turned out to be their pet cat, who kept strutting back and forth behind the heels of the wedding party throughout the entire wedding ceremony, much to the delight of the audience.

On the Miami University campus in Oxford, Ohio, all the men in the wedding party wore kilts the entire day. During the reception, they all got up in front of the guests and did a Scottish-esque dance together. At the end of the dance, they turned their backs to the audience, bent over, and flipped up the back of their kilts, mooning the audience and revealing they were wearing tartan-patterned boxer shorts. It was the hit of the evening!

Another bride and groom rode in to their ceremony on horseback. They dismounted, got married, remounted their horses, and rode off together. I think the bride was into barrel racing.

In Cedar Grove, Indiana, after a Catholic wedding, everyone had already been drinking for a while when one of the young bucks in the wedding party came up to the groom, who was standing right next to me at the time. He said to the groom: "Hey, man, can I try your bride out? Come on, let me try her out!" He repeated this about three times.

Envisioning an upcoming riot, I quickly grabbed the groom by his elbow and said, "I need you to come with me, I've got a couple of photos to take that I need you for." I pulled him away from the scene, the incident became history, and a possible fistfight was avoided. Another super hero incident?

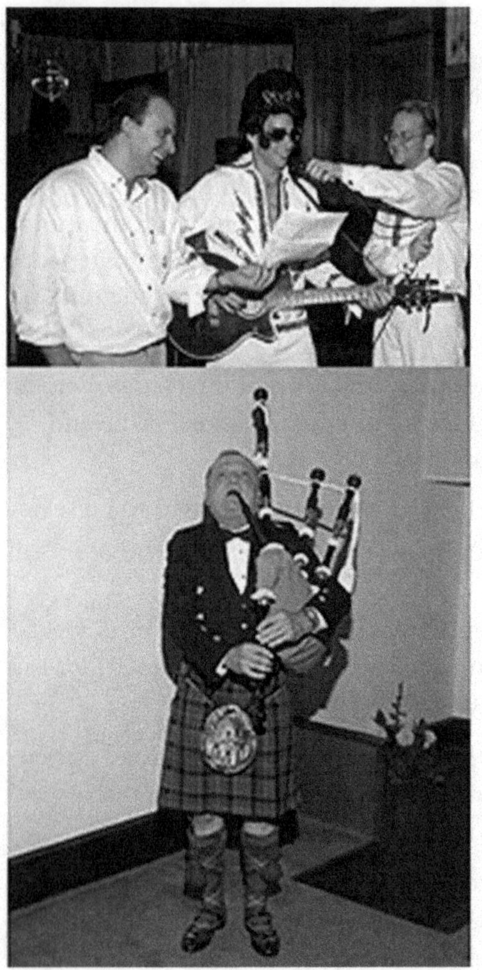

Over the years, I've pretty much seen it all at receptions, from bagpipers to Mexican mariachi bands, to Cajun-style zydeco bands, to a costumed Elvis impersonator complete with Elvis wig who sang to the bride and groom.

There has been a nudist camp in nearby Centerville, Indiana, for as long as I can remember. Either nudists never get married or they decide to take their own photos, but in any event, I never got a call to do any weddings there. I always wondered if the brides would wear wedding gowns or not. Maybe it is a clothing-optional event?

One wedding in Ohio was a couple hours late getting started. One of the bride's relatives was driving from a couple hundred miles away. She was in charge of bringing all the artificial flowers and the altar decorations, and she was late arriving with the goods. We couldn't even take any photos while we were standing around for those couple of hours because we had no flowers!

In Dayton, Ohio, I was standing in the lobby just inside the church's front door, waiting for the wedding party to get ready for the processional. A man wearing a suit came in from outside and two big, burly ushers immediately cut him off. He was told the bride had left specific instructions that he was not to be allowed on the premises. "But I'm her father," the man said. "I've got to see my little girl get married

The ushers refused to allow him to enter and sent him on his way with his hat in his hand. I'm sure there is an interesting story behind what happened. Since I felt I had just witnessed a scene that I shouldn't have, I never inquired about what the details were.

The neatest personalized license plate I ever saw at a wedding belonged to the mother of the bride at a wedding on the campus of Miami University in Oxford, Ohio. It read, "GOTS2GO." I guess she did.

When I arrived in the basement of a church to get photos of the guys getting ready, I found they had all arrived early, were completely dressed and seated around a table playing Texas Hold 'Em poker. I seized the opportunity to get some unique photos, firing away while they played.

Have you ever attended a wedding at a mental institution? Well, on the grounds of Richmond State Hospital, located in Richmond, Indiana, there is a small chapel used for church services for the mental patients there on Sundays. It is also available for weddings, if anyone in your family works at the hospital. I've done weddings there twice. Another connection is that my wife retired from RSH after many years there as a psych attendant.

During one of the weddings there, a few of the mental patients who had grounds privileges wandered into the chapel to watch the wedding from the rear of the building. They caused no trouble, soon lost interest, and went back out on the grounds again after watching for just a few minutes.

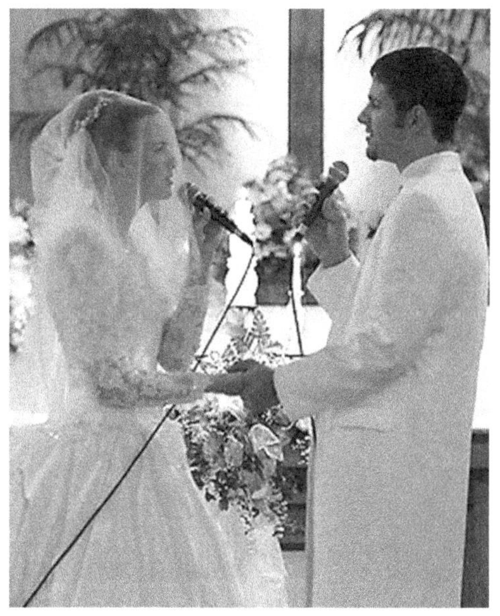

One bride came down the aisle with a remote microphone in her hand under her veil, singing to her groom as she walked. One bride and groom both picked up microphones during their service and sang to each other.

I was thirty minutes into my hour and a half trip to the wedding site when I came to realize that – horror of horrors – I had forgotten to put in my upper denture plate prior to leaving. After making this realization, I debated whether I should go back and get it or go on and do the assignment without it, as I looked anxiously to see how soon the next exit on the interstate would be coming up. Going back to retrieve my denture plate won. I still was able to get the group photos done before the wedding.

The bride's father had started to worry about what was holding me up. He shot me a little bit of a dirty look upon my arrival, but I won his approval for the day by doing a super job of covering all the events that transpired.

Thereafter, I carried a spare upper denture in the glove compartment of my car, so there would never be a repeat of this incident.

Twice, I've done weddings where the bride was the daughter of a couple whose wedding I had photographed twenty years or more before. Now, that's pretty unique! Second generation customers!

The guys in one wedding party had me take a rear view of them all lined up like they were taking a group whiz in the big waterfall in the lobby of the reception hall in Cincinnati. It seems doing so was a custom there.

One set of newlyweds, when introduced at their fancy big city reception, entered smiling, waving – and wearing Mickey Mouse and Minnie Mouse fuzzy slippers which they wore for the rest of the evening.

I have seen all kinds of limos used at weddings over my years in the business, everything from stretch VW bugs and stretch Hummers, to trolley cars, buses, Model T's, and even a 1930's Rolls Royce which I got to ride in later in the day.

One stretch limo I was following to the reception tried to navigate a tight corner at an intersection, but failed to make it. The driver ended up spending five minutes trying to get it around the corner.

Not ten minutes later, the limo driver found himself totally unable to move the limo in any direction. He had gotten the limo hung up in a big dip in the road where two hills came together. None of the limo's wheels were touching the ground and a wrecker had to be called in to free up the limo before anyone in the wedding party could continue on to the reception.

A limo was expected at the bride's home to take the girls in the wedding party to the church, but it never showed up. It had suffered mechanical problems, the owner of the limo service explained to the bride's father. About six cars were quickly pressed into service to get the girls to the church. So much for their planned fancy ride!

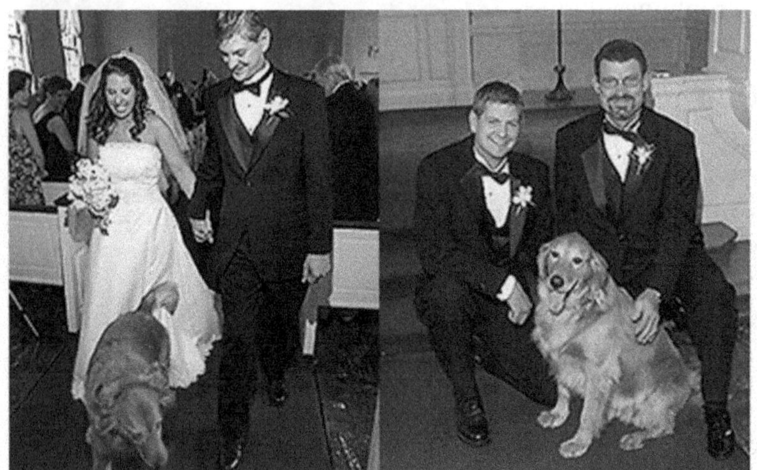

There was a red Labrador who served as "best dog" at a wedding I did about ten years ago between two Miami University students at their on-campus wedding in Oxford, Ohio. The dog eagerly took part in the processional, the recessional, and stood at the altar during the ceremony. It even posed for wedding party group photos afterwards, but I don't remember him attending the reception.

The hottest wedding I ever did took place in a Presbyterian church on the town square in nearby Liberty, Indiana, several years ago. It was a scorcher! Everyone had cherry-red cheeks and sweat dripping from their foreheads and faces as they came down the aisle during the processional. A lot of churches back then didn't have air conditioning.

While waiting to get started photographing a wedding at a small church in Franklin, Ohio, I looked out the window at another church right next door. There was a marquee out front of the other church proudly proclaiming, "Now appearing, live and in person: Jesus Christ."

Some of my wedding workdays were nearly twenty hours long, including six hours driving there, six hours driving home, and eight or more hours of photo coverage. I remember coming from a wedding way up north of Fort Wayne, Indiana. It was after 2 a.m., and I still had two more hours before I would get home, so I had the pedal down.

Suddenly, I saw a police car coming the other way on the divided highway. I tried to slow down, but as soon as he got past me he slammed on his brakes and fishtailed so he was facing back in my direction. He then came charging across the median to get to my side of the road, then flipped on flashing red and blue lights and pulled me over.

He was nice, asking me if I knew I was speeding. I said I had just finished putting in about a twenty-hour day photographing a wedding and reception way up north of Fort Wayne. I told the police officer I was dead tired and just trying to get back to Richmond so I could get to bed before I fell asleep at the wheel.

"Well, I'm going to let you off with just a warning this time. Get home and get some sleep," he said. The same exact scenario transpired about four different times over a six year period. Telling the precise truth always got me off with just a warning.

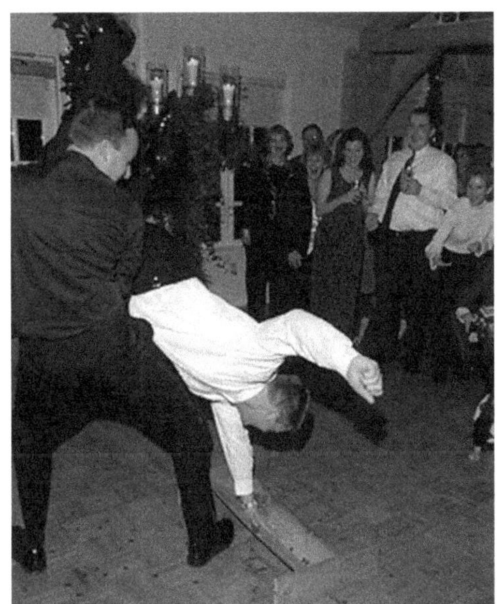

Have you ever seen a Hog Trough Dance at a reception? Neither had I, until I covered a reception in southwestern Ohio. They brought out a six foot long device made to look like a trough hogs from which hogs are fed. The groom danced around and over it, putting first one foot in the trough, then the other. His best man picked him up around the waist and turned him upside down so the groom's head was in the trough. What was it all about, and what inspired the strange dance? Sorry, I still don't have a clue, but it sure made for a bunch of unique photos!

The groom at one wedding I did in the Richmond, Indiana, area was a professional fishing guide in Jackson Hole, Wyoming. When I arrived at the country church in the late morning, the guys were still fishing in the small pond out back of the church.

There would not usually be anyone on site when I arrived at the venue. I would rather get my trip there behind me and have some time on my hands on the other end. I also allotted about an hour and a half extra to cover any delays I might encounter on the way there. Interstates sometimes turn into parking lots!

I learned my lesson about the value and necessity of having time to spare built in to getting to the church on time. It was in the days before GPS, and my route was blocked by a train for a long time. I reached the altar of the twin-spired church in Hamilton, Ohio, just as the first bridesmaid started coming down the aisle. Now that's cutting it close!

One groom had a blindfold slipped on him at the reception, then the fun began. One of the women slipped behind him, putting a paper lei, straw hat, oversized sunglasses and a grass skirt on him, without his knowledge and told him to dance, as the music started up. He did. It wasn't until he got to take the blindfold off, that he discovered how he had be dressed by the woman for everyone's enjoyment.

Looking through the wedding photos I've taken, I just came across some taken at one 2007 reception that jogged my memory about what happened there. What caught my attention was the bewildered and totally embarrassed look on the bride's face in the photo of her, just after the groom removed her garter. The photos preceding this one showed the groom with a disposable camera in his hand.

Next I saw the photo of, I believe, the groom's dad, who was career military officer with lots of campaign ribbons on his uniform. He was auctioning off the camera. These all tied together to jog my memory about this long forgotten, once in a lifetime event. Best I recall, the dad gave the groom the disposable camera right before the groom removed his bride's garter. The groom slipped completely under her gown, with the camera in hand.

He took a photo while under the gown, as everyone saw the flash go off. He then rushed back out and gave the camera to the dad, who had a microphone in hand. The dad proceeded to auction off the camera to the highest bidder, with the photo the groom had taken. I think it brought somewhere between $20 and $50, as there were several anxious male bidders for it. Boys will be boys, I guess?

Even though I could have included those photos in the book, I've decided to just let you use your imagination, instead. I'm sure this bride will applaud my decision to keep her identity a secret.

Half the way through the evening, at a wedding reception in Noblesville, Indiana, the half a dozen bridesmaids were all told to be seated on chairs, in the middle of the dance floor.

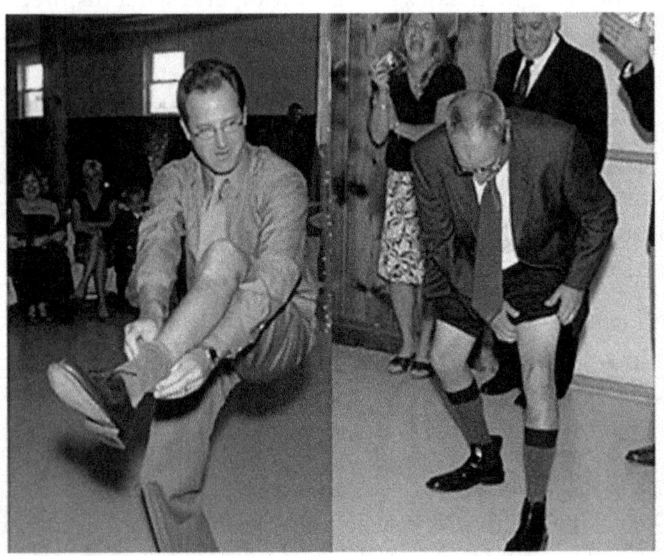

Six or seven men were then drafted from the audience to perform their best raunchy dance in front of the bridesmaids, so those bridesmaids could judge which was the best dancer.

To their credit, all the guys really gave it their best efforts, with many of them rolling up their pant legs to show off their sexy knees, and giving it all they had, dancing back and forth in front of each bridesmaid, in turn, as the music played on. Yup, a rip roaring good time was had by all that night! Sorry, I don't remember who won.

Chapter 13: Health Problems Force Retirement

When I was 57 years old, I realized I was starting to get exhausted by the end of receptions because I was out of shape. I had been guilty of being a couch potato for the past thirty years, and getting older didn't help my health any either!

I decided I wanted to get into shape, so I jumped up off the couch, went outside, and started running regularly. After I had made running a habit, I decided to get competitive. I trained for and ran the Las Vegas Marathon, all 26.2 miles of it, when I was 58.

I remember the following about running the Las Vegas Marathon in the desert:

- running the first half the race behind a guy and his pretty girlfriend, watching her shapely rear end bounce up and down with her every step. It made for some really easy running miles.
- after mile nine, the solid hour of steep downhill running that made my quad muscles tighter than a drum and burn and scream with tremendous pain.
- the 30 mph+ desert headwind sweeping down from the mountains that made me have to work twice as hard to keep my pace in the last half the race.
- stopping to cut a hole in the toe of my shoe at mile ten and still losing a toenail.
- taking a shower after the race, dressing and going out with my wife for a night of winning big at the craps tables.

Locally, I competed in 5k races and came in second in my age group in the Wayne County Challenge, a total points, year-long race competition spanning about eight different races over the course of the year. I went on to finish first in my age group in the Wayne County Challenge both of the next two years. My 5k personal best time was 23:21 at the age of 63, which is the equivalent of running seven minute miles for the entire 3.1 miles: not bad for an old man! I was even faster than a lot of runners in the races who were a quarter century my junior.

In a small 5k race in Losantville, Indiana, I even finished first once, winning the entire race by more than four minutes over the field. Who would have ever thought about winning a race at age 63? I sure was surprised. I was the only competitively trained runner, of any age, who entered this particular race. Everyone else were purely weekend recreational runners and not well-trained. I had passed the halfway turnaround and ran another two minutes, before my nearest competitor came into view running towards me on his way to the turnaround. But hey, regardless of circumstance, I was the first across the finish line by a margin of several minutes and I gladly took the win.

All of this running got me into really good shape, and I never had to worry about becoming exhausted by the end of photographing a reception again. I'm 69 at the time of publication and no longer able to run now due to my health problems, but I still manage to get out and walk four miles nonstop a few times a week.

After professional quality digital equipment had been on the market for about ten years or so, consumer digital equipment got better, too, and much cheaper. Eventually, it seemed like everyone, especially single moms working out of their apartments, thought they could be a pro wedding photographer and were willing to try their hand photographing weddings without any formal training. I read recently they are referred to as "Mamarazzis."

They could more or less fake it by constantly checking the digital display screen on the back of their digital cameras to see if they had the shot or not, each time, before moving on to the next shot. They could adjust their camera settings and shoot it again if they didn't like what they saw on their display screen.

The market in the big cities became glutted with "wedding photographers," and it became really difficult for brides to distinguish who was actually good or professionally trained and who wasn't. During this time, my final couple of years in the industry, the reputation of wedding photography got a black eye, as these wannabes tried to photograph weddings using their consumer-grade equipment, without getting any professional training or having any backup equipment. Maybe this was because the money seemed so easy and therefore looked appealing to them.

These new big city "wedding photographers" were more than happy to undercut even my low prices. The number of weddings I was booking slipped, to the point where I felt the need to semi-retire at 62, start drawing my reduced Social Security, and just do weddings on a bimonthly basis to supplement my Social Security. What a shame. This wasn't planned, it just happened, and I felt I had to roll with the punches in order to survive.

Unfortunately, it seems the very technology I had embraced so early on and which had allowed me to separate myself from my competition had come full circle and backfired against me. Now it had led to my business taking a hard hit.

Wedding photographers are some of the biggest copycats in the world. If a photographer sees a pose he likes and hasn't seen before, he'll claim it as his own creation in a heartbeat. I've done it myself, on occasion. This tendency toward copying other photographers also holds true for any good marketing techniques and business practices.

When I had put everything I was doing online to appear transparent and informative, I had also inadvertently laid the groundwork that made it possible for everyone trying to get into the business to copy everything I was doing.

After a few years of having my poses, marketing and tricks of the trade imitated, especially by new photographers who were in a rush to reach the top of the heap, I was no longer out in front of the pack. Everyone else seemed to be doing the same things now that I had been doing for years.

I seemed to have slipped back to being just a part of the pack again, fighting for clients like a photographer who hadn't been practicing professionally in the area for decades. Potential brides did not know who had copied whom, and really didn't care as long as they got the lowest price for photography services. I was no longer set apart from the crowd, as it seems everyone and his uncle had caught up and was claiming to be a professional wedding photographer.

About this same time, too, one of the top two bridal magazines in the country ran a story advising brides to put off hiring their photographers until the last minute, so the photographers would be panicking about the possibility of not booking that wedding date and would be more willing to bargain with brides on their prices. This was supposedly a foolproof plan for saving brides big money on their wedding photography.

Man, what bad advice! But a lot of brides followed it, and the article was right: it did create panic among the professional photographers throughout the country when bookings really did start to fall off. A lot of professional photographers were really worried about the possibilities of being forced out of business due to this article.

There was an online message board exclusively used by professional photographers– which required you to prove you at least had a wedding photography website and pay about $19 per month in order to gain access to discussions with other pro wedding photographers without worrying about consumers reading it.– The message board was ablaze with photographers worrying about what they were going to do to survive financially because of the effects this one pernicious article was having on their bookings.

Now, let me say: I did not see the magazine or read the article myself, but it seemed like every other wedding photographer in the country had seen it, and they were discussing it extensively, so I got a pretty good idea of the subject matter.

I posted my own concerns on these boards, and another photographer took a pot shot at me with a remark about me being “such a small fish in a big pond I'd hardly be missed.” An Indianapolis photographer came to my defense, saying, "I don't think you understand what's going on here in Indianapolis. Bill Collins is one of the biggest fishes in the Indianapolis pond! We are all suffering."

When I was starting to think seriously about semi-retiring, I contacted a wedding photographer in Indianapolis who had close to a dozen other photographers working for him, to ask if I could work for him, too. His website ranked high on all the major search engines for the Indianapolis wedding photographers search results.

I had told him I was only interested in doing a couple of weddings per month, at most. He said I could work for him on a part-time basis and not have to deal with customers or orders; basically, I would just photograph the wedding using my own equipment and get paid. He said with my experience and reputation he could pay me $750 per wedding, which was a good fee.

I would have taken him up on it, except for the fact he was soon featured on television in Indianapolis in an exposé saying he hadn't delivered any finished wedding albums to clients in well over a year, or possibly it was two years!

I've told you how I produced my albums of my own photos on my digital printer and how I got the finished wedding albums back in the mail the same day I received orders for them. I simply cannot understand how anyone could not deliver the customers' wedding albums. It's the easiest part of the job!

Soon after, I was lying in bed asleep one night, when suddenly I was fully awake, lying on the floor with my forehead hurting and bleeding profusely. I had suffered a mild stroke and it had dumped me on the floor.

I was treated at the hospital in nearby New Castle, Indiana, then transferred by ambulance to Reid Hospital in Richmond, Indiana. After being thoroughly checked over, I finally got to go home.

A couple of months later, I was working on my computer when the left half of the screen suddenly turned entirely blank. I could see the letters on the right half of the screen, but nothing at all on the left half. My wife rushed me to Reid Hospital again, and the doctors there determined I had suffered another mild stroke. It turned out I had a-fib, an irregular heart rhythm, which had thrown a blood clot to my brain after blood had pooled and thickened as a result of the condition in the top part of my heart.

I had come through both mini-strokes, warning shots as I called them, without any serious damage, but I knew my days as a wedding photographer were over. There was just no way I could commit to being at a wedding up to a year in advance when I was suffering strokes which could happen anytime. It was logically time to fully retire.

Another photographer had called me about four years before I retired, offering to buy my website, proweddingphotos.com, because the domain name was ranked in the top ten websites in the world for the keyword "wedding photography." Back then, four years prior, I was using it myself to stay booked and had naturally told him it wasn't for sale, so we never even got around to discussing a price for the site and domain name. Of course, we might have been worlds apart on price, but since it didn't get discussed, we'll never know. I wasn't smart enough to save his contact information.

I had always figured that proweddingphotos.com would probably net me $10,000-$20,000 when I sold it. After I semi-retired, I put up a page on the website offering it for sale to other wedding photographers, as I knew a lot of wedding photographers routinely cruised my site.

Much to my surprise, nobody made an offer to buy it. Keeping the domain name cost me over $100 every four years, so I let it lapse when it came time to renew it again. So much for that anticipated revenue stream!

I have my reduced Social Security to live on now, and I am pretty frugal, as I know how to separate my needs from my wants. I have few needs and even fewer wants, so it doesn't take much money, to keep me happy. My wife is tremendously good at managing money and has taught me about fiscal responsibility over the years, too. So, there really isn't too much to worry about in my retirement, economically.

For the last three years or so, I have been supplementing my personal income by picking up cars for the local Toyota dealership from out-of-town sources and driving them back to the dealership. It pays $10 an hour and gives me pocket money. I make anywhere from $30 to $200 per week working for the Toyota dealer, depending on how many cars they need fetched from out-of-town sources that week. Sometimes, they seem to give me more work than I need or want, but I enjoy doing it and it helps keep me busy and prevents me from getting bored. All is good in my world nowadays.

My heart a-fibrillation, which was probably causing my mini-strokes, was cured with a five hour heart ablation surgery. The doctors cauterized the parts of my heart which were causing the electrical crosstalk between one side of the heart and the other, medically known as a-fib. I've been fine in the cardiology department for over three years now.

Do I miss photographing weddings? I sure enjoyed being able to do it so well, and I do miss getting in the thick of things and dancing the dance wedding photographers do. I've been told I was quite a dancer; I could really get in sync with the natural flow of the day and just go with it.

When I was young, I never received any education about how to handle money. It seemed that I always tried to buy everything I wanted on credit back then. Back when I worked in factories, I would sit around, with pen in hand, when I wanted something, seeing if there was any way I could afford to add in the payments it would take to buy it. I was totally unschooled in how to handle my money. My paycheck was usually gone as soon as I got paid.

When I was in my twenties, I once took my mother with me, as I rode all around town, making my weekly payments I owed. I thought it would show her that I was honorable by making all my payments. Looking back on that now, it makes me feel a little ashamed and embarrassed I was like that back then. Years later, she told me how disappointed she had been that I seemed to owe every merchant in town. I think it kind of broke her heart.

My wife says that I was always a "gadget-guy", who had to have all the latest technology. She was right about that, too. She says that, if I hadn't spent so much money on having all the latest photography equipment, I would probably be a whole lot richer. All told, I would guess that I spend somewhere around a hundred thousand dollars over the years on photography equipment and electronic gadgets.

It wasn't until after I married Sue, that I started to get educated about handling my money. Over the years, she has transformed me into a good money manager, like her.

I got myself totally out of debt about quarter of a century ago and have managed to stay out of debt. I've learned that what you earn isn't nearly as important, in life, as what you do with that money.

I've become a big fan of Suze Ormand and really like the financial advice she gives on her TV show. I just wish that kind of information, about how to handle your money and how to separate my wants from my needs, had been taught to me back when I was in high school. Of course, even if it had been taught, it might have gone right over my head at the time and been totally ignored.

Now that I am semi-retired, I find that I can go in any kind of store, look everything over in the store and come away without having made a single purchase. I have few needs, in retirement, and even fewer wants -- and that pleases me. I think I might have actually matured in that area of my life. Better late than never, I guess. How you treat money sure tells you a lot about yourself.

Allow me to give a great big thanks to all of the couples who hired me over my many years. The clientele who hired me are really who made this book possible. It has been a good ride. I'm glad all you readers out there are getting to come along for this ride down memory lane. I hope you are enjoying it.

Epilogue: I've Decided to "Un-retire"

My granddaughter, Katrina, posted on Facebook at about 1 p.m. yesterday that she was getting married in four hours, surprising everyone. We certainly didn't know we'd be going to a wedding yesterday.

Since I also had her sister, Jessica's, wedding coming up next month, I rushed out and bought a decent digital camera. I managed to get the camera battery charged before the wedding and photographed Katrina and Chuck's wedding for them.

After photographing Katrina's wedding, I realized just how much I missed photographing weddings. It's in my blood and I love doing it. I decided to try to partially "un-retire" and take on about a wedding per month in the Richmond, Indiana, area.

I had a heart ablation almost three years ago, which seems to have solved the problem of my mini-strokes, so I think I'm good to go again, from a health standpoint.

I think I will try to keep it cheap for my new clients, too, charging only about a fifth of what I charged when I photographed weddings for a living. Just for pocket money, you might say. No more twenty-hour workdays photographing weddings far from home!

So, if you know anyone getting married in my area who is looking for a good, affordable photographer with a lot of experience, just have them get in contact me at proweddingphotos@yahoo.com.

You can do me a big personal favor by taking a few seconds to rate and/or review my book on Amazon.com, BarnesandNoble.com and/or Goodreads.com.

I would really appreciate it, because reviews are what drive book sales. After a book has received over thirty favorable reviews from purchasers, Amazon.com seems willing to get behind the book and promote it to their huge client base. Until that book acquires at least thirty good reviews, all the promotional responsibilities fall upon the author alone. Help an author out: leave a review! (See next page for where to leave your reviews/ratings.)

Thanks so much,

Bill

Books by Bill Collins, author

Wedding Photography Improve Quickly

Kindle E-book Edition

http://www.amazon.com/Wedding-Photography-Improve-Quickly-Collins-ebook/dp/B00S41E6IY

Black and White Photo Print Edition [This Edition]:

http://www.amazon.com/Wedding-Photographers-Improve-Quickly/dp/0990487482

Wedding Photographer: a 45 year career

Written as fun read for non-photographer casual readers.

Kindle E-book Edition:

http://www.amazon.com/Wedding-Photographer-45-year-career-ebook/dp/B00OWEYAL0

Black and White Photo Print Edition:

http://www.amazon.com/Wedding-Photographer-45-year-career/dp/0990487458

Full Color Photo Print Edition:

http://www.amazon.com/Wedding-Photographer-45-year-career/dp/0990487466

www.ingramcontent.com/pod-product-compliance
Lightning Source LLC
LaVergne TN
LVHW081325110826
845149LV00007B/1594

9780990487487